Entrepreneur
Guide

How to Start, Manage and Turn-Around

Your Business

Sage Vincent Ikechukwu

Entrepreneur Guide

First Published by Chiysonovelty International 2016

ISBN: 9785317668
ISBN-13: 978-9785317664

Chiysonovelty International
Plot 8 Evule Avenue
Aba,
Nigeria
Email: chiyson@minister.com
Phone: 234-909-227-1088

Printed in the United States of America

Be **E**mpowered **T**o **S**ucceed for entrepreneurship is a way of life. **(BETS)**

CONTENTS

DEDICATION

This book is dedicated to the *Cosmic Divine* – the Infinite Intelligence in the service of humanity for productive living.

PREFACE

In a world where the gap between the rich and the poor keeps widening at a fast rate, it is imperative to x-ray the right key that unlocks the fountain of wealth which the rich uses for wealth accumulation.

The key that unlocks wealth is reflected in Delphic maxim – *"man know thyself,"* in addendum, this wisdom was re-echoed by Confucius when by way of defining the self, he said *"what the superior seeks is in himself; what the small man seeks is in others"* and this is the veritable reliance on the SELF through the application of the will-power to be successful. This self is the fourth factor of economic materialism, now known as Entrepreneurship.

The entrepreneur is the self-made manifest in the economic and business world and this is why we keep hearing the rich say *"I am a self-made billionaire."* More interesting is that globalization has hastened the time it now takes to become a billionaire. To exemplify this point in the words of Robert Kiyosaki, the author of the *Rich Dad Poor Dad* series, he wrote *"In John Rockefeller's day, it took him approximately fifteen years to become a billionaire, he had to acquire many oil wells and create a network of gas stations and gasoline delivery systems. That took a lot of time and a lot of money. Today it would take billions of dollars to build what Rockefeller built. It took Bill Gates approximately ten years to become a billionaire. He had foresight to use IBM's network to grow rapidly. It took Michael Dell and Steve Case, founder of AOL, less than five years to become billionaires. One entrepreneur used the growing demand for computers and the other used the explosive power of the World Wide Web to tap into the power of an explosive network. For each new generation of entrepreneurs, it took less time and less capital to become billionaires, due to the advent of new networks. You too can."*

This shows that the quickest way to wealth creation is through entrepreneurship and this opportunity is available to anyone who is willing to drink from the entrepreneurial chalice. Therefore, the vital question anyone should ask himself or herself is; *Am I willing to become the entrepreneur?* And if I heard you rightly you answered *YES!* So I wish to believe in you and your capacity to become the successful entrepreneur with the delicate idea that will solve the multiplex of world problems.

In commendation, this book is focused on leading anyone in true search of the key that unlocks wealth and serves as a guiding light towards the attainment of the entrepreneurial self. Hence, the chapters are designed to lead and motivate the entrepreneur in achieving purposeful living using the Vinsage Consult signature concept of **BETS** – **B**e **E**mpowered **T**o **S**ucceed for entrepreneurship is a way of life. And so, I am using this inspiring work which has been a beacon of light in the entrepreneurial lifestyle to state that what I have learnt I have applied and what I have applied I have written.

Sage Vincent Ikechukwu

20th September, 2014.

CHAPTER ONE
DEVELOPING THE
ENTREPRENEURIAL IDEA

"You are surrounded by simple, obvious solutions that dramatically increase your income, power, influence and success. The problem is you just don't see them."
– Jay Abraham.

ENTREPRENEURSHIP:
PHILOSOPHY AND PRACTICE

Entrepreneurship is the process of performing the roles of an entrepreneur (*entrep*). It has been defined as the process of planning, operating and assuming the risk of a business venture. It can also be defined as the process of creating a unique value, of pulling together a unique package of resource to exploit an opportunity. The process has been described as going through at least four phases, the conception (*when the would-be entrepreneur perceives an opportunity*), the gestation phase (*when the opportunity is evaluated*), the infancy phase (*when the firm is created*), and the adolescence phase (*where after the firm matures*).

4

While several definitions of entrepreneurship abound, the central idea of the concept incorporates uncertainty and risk-taking, innovation, perception and change. Entrepreneur and entrepreneurship are more often associated with small and medium scale enterprises even though not restricted to them. This is because entrepreneurial endeavours are often given expressions through small and medium-scale enterprises.

Interestingly, the American system of free enterprise has always engendered the spirit of entrepreneurship. America was discovered by entrepreneurs, and the United States of America became a world economic power through entrepreneurial activity. So much as for Africans, who are very entrepreneurial, David Livingstone (*1813-73*) had this to say "*Most of the Africans are natural-born traders; they love trade more for the sake of trading than for what they make by it.*"

Recently, Eric Schmidt, the erstwhile chairman of Google had this to say after touring Africa in 2013: "*... Nigerians are entrepreneurial, stylish, educated... Optimism is appropriate for Africa, as the people we met will do much more with less than we can imagine, and the devices and systems built in the first world will be used in the most creative ways in the emerging new world of Africa.*"

Most importantly and interestingly entrepreneurship is a way of life that has leading edge. And it is in our best interest to know that entrepreneurial engagements are the future and, will be the exclusive and inspiration of creative minds leading to the era of *"creativism"* based on entrepreneurial activity, phasing out capitalism and harnessing the use of resources in different ways that will usher in quantum progress and innovations.

The term entrepreneur is of French origin and was first defined by Richard Cantillon, an Irish-French economist. In his *Essai sur la Nature du commerce en General*, or as in the English translation; Essay on the Nature of Trade in General, he defined an entrepreneur as a person who pays a certain price for a product to resell it at an uncertain price, thereby making decisions about obtaining and using resources while consequently assuming the risk of enterprise. While Cantillon presented the entrepreneur as a risk taker, Jean Say termed the entrepreneur as a planner.

On his part, Jean Baptiste Say, a French economist in his 1803 *Traite d' economic politique*, defined the entrepreneur as one who possessed certain arts and skills of creating new economic enterprises, yet a person who had exceptional insight into society's needs and was able to fulfill them.

In 1848, British economist John Stuart Mill elaborated on the necessity of entrepreneurship in private enterprise. The term entrepreneur subsequently became common as a description of business founders, and the "*fourth factor*" of endeavour was entrenched in economic literature as encompassing the ultimate ownership of a commercial enterprise.

This concept appeared first in 1437 in the French dictionary; *Dictionnaire de la langue Francaise* (*and later re-appeared in the French merchant dictionary; Dictionnaire Universel de Commerce which was edited by Jacques des Bruslon and published in 1723*) and it defined an entrepreneur as a person who is active and gets things done. A person that is willing to risk life and fortune.

The early reference to the entrepreneur in the 14th century spoke about tax contractors: individuals who paid a fixed sum of money to a government for the licence to collect taxes in their region. The word itself, from the 17th century French "*entreprendre,*" refers to individuals who were "*undertakers,*" meaning those who "*undertook*" the risk of new enterprise. They were "*contractors*" who bore the risk of profit or loss, and many early entrepreneurs were soldiers of fortune, adventurers, builders, merchants, and, incidentally, funeral directors.

In the 19th century, entrepreneurs were the "captains of industry, the risk takers, the decision makers, the individuals who aspired to wealth, those who gathered and managed resources to create new enterprises. Entrepreneurship is one of the four mainstream economic factors: land, labour, capital and entrepreneurship."

An entrepreneur has also been defined as an independent business individual who efficiently and effectively combines the four factors of production. Those factors are land (*natural resources*), labour (*human input into production using available resources*), capital (*any type of equipment used in production i.e. machinery*) and enterprise (*intelligence, knowledge and creativity*).

Another definition of the entrepreneurs as given by the World Bank is that they are people who perceive profitable opportunities, are willing to take risk in pursuing them and have the ability to organize a business.

Entrepreneurs are persons who are ingenious and creative in finding ways that add to their own wealth, power and prestige.

Entrepreneurs are people who have the ability to see and evaluate business opportunities; to gather the necessary resources to take advantage of them; and to initiate appropriate action to ensure success.

And in support of this position the political economics have said that, entrepreneurship is the process of identifying and starting a new business venture; sourcing and organizing the required resources while taking both the risks and rewards associated with the venture.

Furthermore, according to Joseph A. Schumpeter, *"the entrepreneur is an innovator, who introduces a new product or service, opens a new market or develops a new marketing system, directs the appropriation of resources as well as the organization of new industry."*

Schumpeter further posited that the entrepreneur's driving force among others is hinged either on the desire to found a private dynasty, the will to be competitive or the sheer joy of creation could dominate the entrepreneur's judgement.

On his part, the management pundit, Peter Drucker posited that *"an entrepreneur searches for change, responds to it and exploits opportunities. Innovation is a specific tool of an entrepreneur hence an effective entrepreneur converts a source into a resource."*

An entrepreneur is a risk-taker in the private enterprise system, a person who seeks a profitable opportunity and takes the necessary risks to set up and operate a business. Many entrepreneurs start their business from scratch, but you don't have to launch your own company to be considered an entrepreneur.

Consider Ray Kroc, founder of McDonald's. He started by buying a small hamburger shop and he grew this small venture into a multibillion-dollar global business.

Entrepreneurs and Business Owners

Entrepreneurs differ from many small business owners. Although many small business owners possess the same drive, creative energy and desire to become big-business owners, others may be content to operate a business that provides a comfortable living. By contrast, the typical entrepreneur tries to make the business grow.

Entrepreneurs combine their ideas and drive with

money, employees and other resources to create a business that fills a market need. That entrepreneurial role can make something significant out of a small beginning.

Usually, the start-up years are the most difficult and tempting time to quit for the entrepreneurs often because he or she is often unknown and barely breaks through, seems a loner and forsaken or confused.

Those who know him hardly understand and comprehend his vision and where he is going but he must be self-motivated to sail through for the limit of self-awareness is the limit he can attain and finally when success comes he becomes an achiever and the man of the people.

The entrepreneur (*or an entrep*) according to Sage Vincent Ikechukwu, Principal Consultant at Vinsage Consult *"is one who probes for opportunities to create and manage life ventures (business), taking responsibilities for the calculated risks and balanced gains (prestige and freedom). For the entrepreneur each day is a challenge as well as an opportunity for wealth, it allows for the freedom to pursue one's own vision, the grace to earn above salaried workers and the flexibility and control over one's time and finances."*

The be-all and end-all of the entrepreneur is:

E – **E**xamines life's opportunities.

N – **N**urtures the vision.

T – **T**reats everyone as a prospective customer.

R – **R**esolves any differences in wants.

E – **E**stablishes priorities and roadmaps.

P – **P**repares for any eventualities.

R – **R**esists the urge to backslide.

E – **E**spouses confidence in the vision.

N – **N**egotiates the way through.

E – **E**fficiently discharges his duty.

U – **U**ses resources to achieve the vision.

R – **R**eceives reward for calculated risks.

From the above concept of an entrepreneur, it is easy to understand the position of an entrepreneur and to appreciate their important role in the economy. Similarly, at Harvard University, entrepreneurship has been expressed on the dynamics of creation and innovation, this has become known as the Harvard tradition on entrepreneurship.

The Harvard Tradition

These ideas were developed at the Research centre in Entrepreneurial History at Harvard University. The researchers agreed that entrepreneurship consisted of three dimensions:

a) Changes in economic system.

b) Creation of organizations for the commercialization of innovation.

c) Task of entrepreneur: create profits (*Landstrom, 1999:10*).

Another Scholar, Howard Stevenson of the Harvard Business School, identified entrepreneurship as the pursuit of opportunity without regard to resources currently controlled (*Howard H. Steveson, 1975*).

ENTREPRENEURS AND MANAGERS

Entrepreneurs can work in organizations as Intrapreneurs, that is, an entrepreneurially oriented person who develops innovations and make changes happen within the company. While managers are persons who acquired competence and skills from their experience and training as such direct the activities of others and the organization's resources.

Entrepreneurs differ from managers, for managers are employees who direct the efforts of others to achieve an organization's goals. In the case of small start-up firms, owners may find it necessary to serve as owner-managers to implement their plans for the business and to offset human resource limitations at the fledgling company.

Entrepreneurs may also perform a managerial role, but their overriding responsibility is to use the resource of their organizations – employees, money, equipment and facilities to accomplish their goals.

Particularly, in the start-up stage of a new venture, entrepreneurs pursue their ideas for business success and take the initiative to find and organize the resources they need to start and build their ventures.

Bill Gates recognized his own entrepreneurial role at Microsoft when he resigned from the Chief Executive post of his now-giant enterprise to take on the position of *"Chief Software Architect."*

The change enabled Microsoft's former Chief Executive Officer (*CEO*), Steve Ballmer to focus on managing the company while Gates looks for new business opportunities, (*with the arrival of the incumbent Microsoft CEO, Satya Nadella, it is expected that he would also refocus the company with a strategy that is mobile-cum-data centric while making further acquisitions*).

Also, Microsoft's growth has come not from Gate's talents as a programmer – most people agree that Microsoft's programs usually borrow existing ideas – but his savvy is in deploying resources to build a strong market for his products. The measure of Gates' success as an entrepreneur is the hugely profitable business he built by developing markets for operating systems and business software.

Bill Gates used existing ideas to build on the success of his company having realized the importance of Bernice Fritz-Gibb's words, *"Creativity often consists of merely turning up what is already there."* Many entrepreneurs can make maximum use of their creative energy by turning up what is in existence in a new profitable mechanism through a marketing system that would be a pace-setter.

CHAPTER TWO
THE ENTREPRENEUR
PERSONALITY

"An appealing personality is not something grafted on from without. It is not like a coat of paint applied to a building or cosmetics used on the face. It is expressed through the body, the mind, the heart and spirit. Although some persons seem to have been born with an exceptionally appealing personality, no one has a monopoly of it." – Edith Johnson

Studies of entrepreneurs have identified certain personality's traits and behaviours common to them that differ from those required for managerial success.

One of these traits is the willingness to assume the risk involved in starting a new venture. Some employees leave their job to start their own companies and become successful entrepreneurs. Others find that they lack the characteristics required to start and grow a business.

TYPES OF ENTREPRENEURS

Entrepreneurs are action-oriented, highly motivated individuals who take risks to achieve goals and apply their talents in different situations. The three basic types are as follows:

a) Classic entrepreneurs.

b) Intrapreneurs.

c) Change Agents or Turnaround entrepreneurs

A. Classic Entrepreneurs

These entrepreneurs identify business opportunities and allocate available resources to tap those markets. The story of Ari B. Horowitz exemplifies the actions of a classic entrepreneur.

Horowitz declares that he is *"in the business of building businesses."* In the first decade after earning his college degree, he started or led the growth of five companies, most of them serving high-tech industries in the United States.

Horowitz looks for markets that have large potential, and then seeks an advantage through speed, relying on his drive and selling ability to quickly assemble the money and people needed to serve those markets.

For example, Horowitz started Gray Peaks, a consulting firms specialized in high-tech business. While he was still managing that company, he realized that the demands of hiring and managing skilled employees presented another opportunity which is providing that service to other companies.

So Horowitz began Opus 360 corp. to provide an online service called FreeAgent.Com, which matches independent consultants with clients and enables business track employee's work on individual projects.

This typifies the classic entrepreneur, who is always and often on the look-out for business opportunities and perceptive in analyzing a real investment.

B. Intrapreneurs

These set of experts are entrepreneurially oriented people who seek to develop new products, ideas and commercial ventures within large organizations.

Today's fast changing business climate compels large firms to innovate continually to maintain their competitive advantages.

To do this the company's hiring process has to be designed on personality profile to support innovative individuals for entrepreneurial activities as it helps retain valuable employees who might want to leave their jobs to start their own businesses.

The company is expected to implement a system that allows personal freedom to explore new products and technologies for fast market-place winners in addition to traditional product development.

Intrapreneurship needs managerial commitment to succeed, and once management has approved the overall strategy, intrapreneurship can flourish and raise new levels of innovation, more profitable ventures, commercially viable expansion projects and also reposition the organization as the industry leader.

C. Change Agents or Turnaround Entrepreneurs

These set of professionals are managers who seek to revitalize established firms to keep them competitive in today's market place.

They bring in to bear that entrepreneurial mindset needed to put the moribund or on the brink of bankruptcy organization back to life.

Change agent entrepreneurs have that *"Midas touch"* to revitalize any organization that is on the verge of folding up.

The Subsets of Entrepreneurs

Entrepreneurs abound in different sectors of the

economy and can be identify by the nature and context of what they do in the market place.

Description	Sector
Entrepreneurs	Enterprise
Infopreneur	Data and information
Netpreneur	Internet/web based (*e.g. Google, Facebook, Amazon*)
Agropreneur	Agriculture (*Green economy*)
Sportpreneur	Sports
Investopreneur	Investment/venture capital (*e.g. Warren Buffet*)
Media-preneur	Media (*e.g. Oprah Winfrey, Rupert Murdoch*)
Sociopreneur	Social services (*e.g. Florence Nightingale, Mary Montessori*)

Entrepreneurs are visionaries with passion for practical realization of their vision. And irrespective of the industry they find themselves, the entrepreneurs bring passion and drive into action. Money is not the primary object that motivates entrepreneurs, for it is the craving to put ideas to serve a need because every corporation is the seed of an entrepreneurial idea.

WHY BECOME AN ENTREPREPRENEUR

Entrepreneurship is taught in universities and governments push for economic reforms to drive entrepreneurial activities yet it is a personal decision an individual has to make. Some individuals like the hype and claim it as title while this is acceptable it must go beyond rhetoric and sheer grandiloquence.

Some individuals are motivated by high unemployment, some become entrepreneurs by the dissatisfaction of working for someone, and some individuals become entrepreneurs to escape unreasonable bosses or unreasonable salary and rewards.

While some believe their ideas are worth a trial and represent an unmet demand or a business opportunity that is needed in the market place. Primarily, entrepreneurs are motivated by four reasons:

a) Desire for independence or being in control.

b) Desire for financial freedom.

c) Desire for job security.

d) Desire to improve societal quality of life.

A. Desire for Independence or Being in Control

Desire for independence or Being in control is the *"I want to be able to do my own thing and be in charge of my affairs."* It is the desire to take responsibility for whatever you do and be comfortable doing what you like and want to do.

This is self-management, that is, of not having to take excuse to be yourself. More-so, it is driven by the thrill of the independence of when you work, how you work, where you work and why you work, without you having to look over your shoulders.

Being independent as your own boss allows the freedom to live one's life, on one's standards than one could as an employee.

B. Desire for Financial Freedom

Naturally, entrepreneurs are wealth creators. As an employee you only live within your salary and wait for the next pay-check. No company would pay his or her employee an amount that can be enough to provide all his or her needs.

The iron law of wages states that *"real wages always tend, in the long run, toward the minimum wage necessary to sustain the life of the worker."* Wages tend toward a level sufficient only to maintain a subsistence.

Meaning obviously that under this economic law and reality, you can never earn enough from your pay check to set yourself free financially.

Entrepreneurs create profitable business and get to keep the financial gains to themselves. As an employee before a company pays you $5000 monthly, the company must be making more than $5000.

Entrepreneurs know that being entrepreneurial has its financial reward and can take a little patience and even years but it is more fulfilling than having to work for someone's else pocket.

C. Desire for Job Security

Job security is guaranteed for an entrepreneur for he owns the job and cannot be sacked or fired. When employees hear of downsizing and layoff, there is tension for no one is safe or immune to dismissal.

Know that many unemployed persons are gunning for your position and graduates of competence are coming to the labour market in thousands, and there is a large pool to draw labour from even from retirees.

The biographies and stories of successful men and women, talks of individuals who did not sit in one place for monthly wages but individuals who were prepared to take the risk to start something worthwhile even with little or no finance. For having no university education or financial support should not be an excuse to live from hand to mouth.

You may have heard that your background has no right or justification to put your back on the ground, this is because in the order of nature, man is no prisoner of his environment, and the environment is of no hindrance to a man's potential or what he can achieve as nature responds to the greed and need of man.

Therefore, I say it loud and clear that it is the inability to develop oneself that is the hindrance to what a man can achieve unless he commits himself to the task. Hence, any lazy or wretched man is a slave of conformity to unfounded myths, occasioned by negative traditions and consolidated by complacence – derived primarily from his indecision.

An entrepreneur's job depends, not on the decisions of employees, but on the decisions of customers and investors and on the cooperation and commitment of the entrepreneur's own employees. This makes entrepreneurship the best insurance on job security.

D. Desire to Improve Societal Quality of Life

Entrepreneurship is an attractive career option for people seeking to improve the quality of their lives and to make a meaning in peoples' lives by employing those who cannot start a business and satisfy peoples' need. Entrepreneurship gives a sense of fulfillment.

Interestingly, knowing that you are contributing to the quality of life with your product and services guarantees, the entrepreneur a level of inner happiness that can only be gotten by individuals who are making life more enjoyable for others. Surely making life better for others is an unquantifiable reward for entrepreneurship.

CHAPTER THREE

BUILDING

ENTREPRENEURIAL SKILLS

"Happiness comes when we test our skills towards some meaningful purpose." – John Stossel

CHARACTER TRAITS OF ENTREPRENEUR

Every person is a unique individual, and no two persons are alike. Different people have different experiences in life. They are living in different life situations with different commitments and responsibilities and they also have different life goals.

John Hornaday of Bason College was among the first to use surveys and intense interviews to develop a composite list of entrepreneurial traits. These traits include:

- Self-confident and optimistic.
- Able to take calculated risk.
- Respond positively to challenges.
- Flexible and able to adapt.
- Knowledgeable of markets.
- Able to get along well with others.
- Independent minded.

- Versatile knowledge.

- Energetic and diligent.

- Creativity.

- Need to achieve.

- Dynamic leader.

- Responsive to suggestions.

- Take initiatives.

- Resourceful and persevering.

- Perceptive with foresight.

- Responsive to criticism.

These traits provide a critical support for the survival of the entrepreneur. Having some of the traits listed above is an invitation to become an entrepreneur and to learn others, for the true entrepreneur is the person who constantly invests in learning and grows through information and research.

Having positive attitudes and a healthy self-image is essential for all entrepreneurs because being successful as an entrepreneur depends on your willingness to accept responsibility for your own work, pursue goals related to your skills and abilities and also, realize that acceptable results are more important than perfect results.

The difference between successful individual and the unsuccessful ones is that successful individuals do not have the best alternative rather they have the adaptable alternative and are flexible, including having an open mind to learning.

These characteristics are the building blocks of entrepreneurs, as it does help distinguish the entrepreneurs from the pack and set them on the part of success.

For success to be fulfilling, you as an entrepreneur must **B**elieve **I**n **S**omething (**BIS**) and see the success journey as:

S – **S**et appropriate goals.

U – **U**se your optimum talents and gifts.

C – **C**onnect with the people you need.

C – **C**omplete your tasks on time.

E – **E**xceed the mediocrity.

S – **S**elect the adaptable alternative without regrets.

S – **S**ee that you keep succeeding with your goal.

The skills' uniqueness that sharpen the entrepreneur for success include:

1. Vision.
2. Creativity.

3. Need to achieve.

4. High level of Energy.

5. Self-confidence and optimism.

6. Tolerance of failure.

7. Internal locus of control.

8. Simplicity in ambiguity.

9. Risk taking.

1. Vision

Wealth is a consequence of smart working visionaries. Earlier we agreed that entrepreneurs are visionaries with passion for practical realization of their vision. This is so true for entrepreneurs must visualize where they want to be and how to get there.

Vision is insight, which means looking inward into the well spring of your individuality. Where your vision is, there is your power and only you have to believe in it before others can rally around you, this is because where there is vision there is provision without division to envision the mission on revision so that you do not miss the mission or omit the fission of positioning to reposition for the remission of recession.

Hence, the entrepreneur pictures the dream's essence, sees the vision, set the mission, go the values, run the reason and finish the purpose.

Entrepreneurs begin with a vision, an overall idea for how to make their business idea a success and then they passionately pursue it. Bill Gates and Paul Allen launched Microsoft with the vision of a computer on every desk and in every home, all running Microsoft software.

Their vision helped Microsoft to become the world's largest marketer of computer software. It guided the company and provided clear direction for employees as Microsoft grew, adapted and prospered in an industry characterized by tremendous technological change.

At Amazon.com, vision has helped entrepreneur Jeff Bezos to lead his employees through the turbulent birth of internet economy. Bezos' vision is of a *culture of customer obsession.* When his company was just two years old, it faced its first major competition, as Barnes & Nobles entered the internet marketplace for books.

People questioned whether Amazon could survive against an experienced book retailer. Bezos told Amazon employees that they should *wake up terrified every morning but to be very precise what they are terrified of.* And that, he said, should be the company's customers, the people with whom the company had an important relationship with. Bezos uses his role as a visionary to keep employees focused on what would enable the company to continue growing in a more competitive environment.

Clearly, visions are ideas for a better world and ideas position entrepreneurs for the mission. These three words VISION, IDEA and MISSION are so strong and vital to entrepreneurs for organizations are tools in the hands of those who set them up and every organization should possess these three basic and critical components, for these are the root system that nourishes and sustains the organization.

The **V.I.S.I.O.N** explains:

V – Valuable

I – Imagination

S – Satisfyingly

I – Improving the

O – Objectives of

N – Necessity.

The **V.I.S.I.O.N** which as stated above is valuable imagination satisfyingly improving the objectives of necessity, clearly makes for proper understanding of what a vision truly is. It is the ability to visualize with the mind of a state that is presented in patterns and can be experienced.

This is the insight required to progress and succeed due to the fact that it taps the resources of the mind and illuminates the process of achieving the goal. Vision is the vehicle of the truth which is the wholeness of the organization or an individual.

Understandably, since it is the ability to see with the mind, the mind is a repository of valuable resources, it facilitates the imagination and projections of what is, and ought to be and can be, as it translates words, thoughts, expressions in a mechanics that levitate the psychic into patterns or graphically comprehensible picture perfect of what the human being can accomplish and thus produce a sense of purpose.

It is germane to stress that this vision is the use or the application of the mind to express meaning and raise an awakeness toward achieving something worthwhile.

It is on this premise that one can say that vision is not the use of the eyes to see, for it is wise to say that vision is seeing beyond what the eyes could not, and that is why primarily when people want to think of an awakeness or visualize, the eyes are often closed so that the mind can function optimally. It is this capacity that sets the entrepreneur as a visionary who also demonstrates ability to follow through with the vision.

Therefore, when the entrepreneur visualizes of a world-class brand of his or her new product or service, he understands where the venture is headed. This enables the entrepreneur to step in, when the employees or team get stuck in the project, this reminds one of Steve Jobs.

Steve Jobs was a visionary in the computing industry. At the age of twenty-one (21), he co-founded Apple computers in 1976, revolutionizing the look and feel of computing with the Apple Macintosh. As the company grew and became a force in the industry, Steve Jobs became dissatisfied with the way the Board of Directors led the company so he resigned in May, 1985 to pursue other interests and found other companies like Pixar Inc and NeXT. The Apple Company floundered and was on the verge of bankruptcy under its new management.

The Apple Company had to turn back to its visionary – Steve Jobs for direction and assistance, and reinstated him as the CEO. Steve Jobs once again, refocused the

Apple Company, set it on the part of innovation with well diversified investments including the Apple IPhone which helped repositioned the Apple Inc as a successful company it is today. Without doubt, it was vision that enabled Steve Jobs to understand the next step of the whole picture.

Another example of a visionary is Henry Ford, the founder of Ford Motors. When he was constructing the famous *"T-model,"* he was once told by his team of engineers that the model was not possible because they could not imagine how. It may interest you to know that these engineers were professionals vast in their expertise but they lacked vision. Henry Ford was not moved by their profound and vast experience as engineers but he insisted on constructing the model.

Henry Ford's insistence was based on the model being improved on the objectives of necessity which is reflected in his assertion that; *"I will build a car that is for the great multitude. It will be large enough for the family, but small enough for the individual to run and care for. It will be constructed of the best materials, by the best men to be hired, after the simplest designs that modern engineering can devise. But it will be so low in price that no man making a good salary will be unable to own one – and enjoy with his family the blessing of hours of pleasure in God's great open spaces."*

Owing to Henry Ford's vision, he implemented a fast technique of mass production which made it possible to assemble a *"T-model"* car in every ninety-three (93) minutes as such revolutionized the car-manufacturing industry and made cars accessible to the middle class.

By the year 1918, more than half of the cars in America were the T-model cars; this development enabled more Americans to own cars. What is more, it was vision that enabled Mr. Ford to understand the necessity of the project as such it is imperative for entrepreneurs and organizations to have a clearly written vision statement that helps to project and lead them through the phases of growth, financial stress and prosperity.

In précis, for the vision of any venture to be successful, the valuable imagination should satisfyingly be improved on the objectives of necessity. It is said that *"vision helps companies to unify the actions of far-flung divisions, keep customers satisfied, and sustain growth"* because *"vision is only the first step along an organization's path to success."*

The next component of the organization is IDEA. For now, we will focus on an idea being seed of creativity and then deal with the concept of IDEA under Creativity while the third component of an organization's tripod which is MISSION would be treated under High Energy Level.

2. Creativity (*key image of capacity to project service experience*)

Creativity is a virtue of entrepreneurs who conceive new ideas for goods and services, and bring forth innovative ways to navigate and surmount difficult problems and situation. Creativity in the words of Brewster Ghiselin is *"The ability to create meaningful ideas, forms and methods; the process by which one utilizes creative ability; originality of thought, expression; imagination. The inventor whether artist or thinker, creates the structure of his psychic life by means of his work."*

From the above definition, the entrepreneur in this context is one who is creative, by utilizing his or her creative ability, imagination, meaningful ideas, methods or systems to create worthy and strategic new enterprises, business innovations and productive ventures. It also includes the ability to build new platforms and structures or marketing systems to sell his or her product or services.

Creativity is the ability to bring forth something into existence that is to say that creativity is a coinage of two words; *"creative"* and *"ability"* which implies the key image of capacity to project service experience. The point that needs to be highlighted is on *"ability"* and not *"activity."* It helps to distinguish the entrepreneur from a businessman who works for the creativity of entrepreneurs.

The entrepreneur creates, manufactures or establishes the product and services that the business-people *"buy and sell."* The entrepreneur establishes the company which owns the stocks that people buy and sell at the stock-market.

In this set-up, stockbrokers are business-people, the agents of the entrepreneur who are busy trading to multiply the income of the company owner (*stakeholder*), thereby making the entrepreneur wealthier.

Creativity according to Boone and Kurtz; is the capacity to develop novel solutions to perceived organizational problems. Creativity refers to the ability to sell better by improving the ways of doing business.

This ability is in the capacity and the creative capacity is encapsulated in the concept C.R.E.A.T.E to mean:

C – **C**ontent is the key of originality.

R – **R**eality is the image of possession.

E – **E**nergy is the capacity to sustain purpose.

A – **A**spiration is the projection of actionable idea.

T – **T**ransformation is the service of the convinced mind.

E – **E**xcellence is the experience through overcame difficulty.

The social scientists agree on five stages of the creative process; they are as follows:

- Idea Germination.
- Preparation.
- Incubation.
- Illumination.
- Verification.

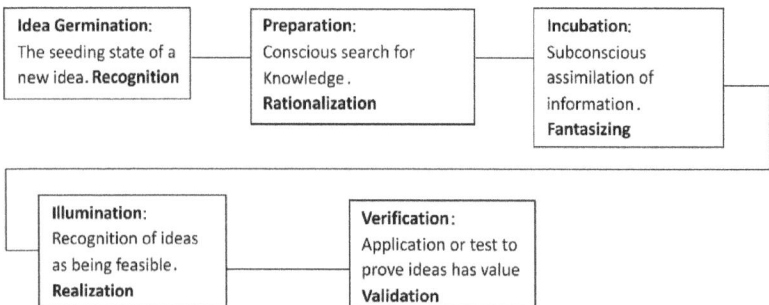

Idea Germination: The seeding state of a new idea. **Recognition**	Preparation: Conscious search for Knowledge. **Rationalization**	Incubation: Subconscious assimilation of information. **Fantasizing**

Illumination: Recognition of ideas as being feasible. **Realization**	Verification: Application or test to prove ideas has value **Validation**

A model of the creative process (*McOliver et al 2008*)

Creativity is an ability that individuals can recognize; any individual who exposes himself or herself to the influence of creativity is not far from being creative. Neuro-scientific research has shown in the PloS ONE study that there is no difference between brain hemispheres no matter how creative or logical you are. This is against popular myths that people that are left brained excel in logical thinking while right brained individuals are more creative. Anyone can be creative by:

- Probing problems for opportunities for problems are guidelines not stop-signs.
- Having wild imaginations.
- Thinking of alternative choices even wild choices can be a source of innovation.
- Using opposite attraction (*e.g. bread and butter, pen and paper*).
- Mixing composite (*relating different parts to form one unique whole*).
- Asking questions for clarity and discernisation.
- Reversing angle approach (*going against the traffic i.e. against accepted order*).
- Reversing engineering / re-engineering.
- Detailing of simple things.

- Mood mocking and directional deciphering.
- Thinking of how to make common ideas, process and projects to become uncommon and vice versa.
- Writing down your ideas with an open mind.
- Deliberately viewing things up-side down.
- Being curious and investigate how things are done and practice recreating them.
- Making a mis-match of things and observe any uniqueness or blending.
- Steering your thinking in using what works in another field, industry or sector and apply it to another field.
- Engaging in regular mental and physical exercises.
- Meditating often and build concentration.

The process of creativity can be dug up from problems. Typically, problems are dreaded but problems are changes that arise as perceived threats which refines for competitive necessity. They produce opportunities for profit as opportunities are hidden in problems. Get this straight, problem is the mother of creativity, everything created starts from the womb of problems.

Creativity is not the exclusive reserve of any individual as long as one can learn and think constructively. It is ideas that drive creativity and creativity does not go out of fashion. Remember idea is the seed of creativity. Ideas are treasures of a positive minded individuals and do not come cheap hence Todd Gitlin said, *"Ideas have consequences."* It is also true that this fast modern world where individuals are constantly wearing their thinking caps, ideas has become so useful that it is no longer about having an idea but how fast you do implement the idea that matters.

Mark Zukerberg and Dustin Moskovitz, the founders of Facebook were not the first to have the idea of social network with faces and photos, in-fact, it resulted in a lawsuit by Cameron Winklevoss, Tyler Winklevoss and Divya Narenda whose ideas were used to program Facebook, eventually it was settled by Mark Zukerberg with 1.2 million shares worth $300 million at Facebook's IPO.

Even the word Facebook was borrowed from the book given to students at the start of the academic year to help students know about each other. So an idea need not be out of reach but should be applicable. Little wonder American prolific inventor, Thomas Edison (*having 1,093 US patents to his name*) said *"Your ideas has to be original in its adaptation to the problem you are working on."*

I.D.E.A

An **IDEA** means

I – **I**gniting

D – **D**iscovering

E – **E**xpressing

A – **A**wesomeness.

For ideas are like diamonds

Rough – Polish it

Hidden – Find it

Solid – Trust it

Hard – Value it

Treasure – Protect it

Jewellery – Flaunt it

Quality – Insure it

Costly – Acquire it

Attitude – Respect it

Freedom – Live it

Bright – Show it

Ecstasy – Savour it

Beautiful – Admire it

Jealousy from others – Laugh it off

Diamonds are forever – Ideas are everlasting.

Therefore, *"Do not study the idea to death with experts and committees, get on with it, and see if it works."* – Kenneth Iverson

Another point that has to be considered under this subject is innovation which is a subset of idea and is often refined through creative engagements. The management guru, Peter Drucker recognized this when he said that; *"Innovation is the specific instrument of entrepreneurs."*

There is a little difference between creativity and innovation, although they are often used as same. However, innovation is the process of doing new things. It is the bringing forth or the introduction of what already exist in a new and different way.

Innovation puts to usefulness an idea, a new method or system into practical and workable usage which usually take the form of making a prototype or the adaptation of an old product, applying an idea or influence from another field to better an existing product, service or system so as to serve a technological or socio-economic need.

Furthermore, Amar Bhidé, the author of *The Origin and Evolution of New Businesses*, posited that *"This innovation rarely takes place in major leaps but in small steps, as entrepreneurs try out small modifications of the status quo and abandon any ideas the market rejects."*

According to National Commission on Entrepreneurship (*NCOE*) in the United States of America, *"By one count, entrepreneurs are the force behind two-thirds of inventions and ninety-five percent of major innovations made since World War Two."*

This research further demonstrates the important role of the entrepreneurs in the economy and the impact they make in the society. One cannot be mistaken to say that the purpose of innovation is to enable the continual usefulness, competence, relevance and to act as a source of critical support in being successful in the marketplace.

The entrepreneur can maximize the profitability of his or her company through how innovative the company is. This innovation can come from both internal and external sources.

Internal sources come from new company goals,

production problems, ineffective marketing programme, employees' complaints and employees' participation in proffering new solutions. While the external sources for innovation can come from developments in foreign or the international market, customers' enquiry and feedback, socio-economic trends, technological advancements and natural phenomena.

The entrepreneur that is innovative knows that innovation involves critical thinking. Boone and Kurtz in their book, *Contemporary Business* did define critical thinking as the ability to analyse and assess information in order to pinpoint problems or opportunities.

The critical thinking process includes activities like determining the authenticity, accuracy and worth of information, knowledge and arguments available. It involves looking beneath the surface for deeper meaning and connections that can assist in identifying critical issues and solutions.

Critical thinking encourages the entrepreneur to look beneath the surface of what has been made, identify vital issues, discover and offer solutions through the application of the concept of **I.N.N.O.V.A.T.I.O.N**

Below are the meaning of **I.N.N.O.V.A.T.I.O.N**

I – Increase the velocity of doing things with ease.

N – Never dwell with the mediocrity.

N – Newest improvement comes in simplicity.

O – Observe what needs to be done as done.

V – Vary with the accepted norm.

A – Arrive with a solution offering.

T – Take precaution in motion without movement.

I – Integrate functions with new or existing structures.

O – Orderly principle is better than avowed procedure.

N – Never give in to, it is not possible.

The entrepreneur can introduce innovation by the

- Use of existing structures with or for new functions.
- Use of existing functions with or for new structures.
- Use of new structures with or for new functions.

To draw the curtain, entrepreneurs can distinguish themselves by means of being creative and sustain the enterprise by being innovative. This point is made quite understandable with the words of Theodore Levitt, *"creativity is thinking new things, innovation is doing new things."* The word *"thinking"* and *"doing"* determines the relationship for long term success.

As Henry Ford once said *"the man who has the largest capacity for work and thought is the man who is bound to succeed."* And to quote Peter Drucker once more, *"innovation is the transformation of creative ideas into useful applications but creativity is a prerequisite to innovation."*

Entrepreneurs often achieve success by making creative improvements rather than single-handedly revolutionizing an industry.

Amar Bhidé's research identified a substantial amount of creativity among entrepreneurs *"at the tactical level"* – in other words, in the ways entrepreneurs built their business, more so than in the product itself.

Successful entrepreneurs tend to be creative in how they get attention from prospective investors or customers and in the ways they build trust in the absence of a proven track record.

3. Need to Achieve

Naturally, entrepreneurs make things happen instead of hoping on luck and chance because they are competitive and self-motivated. This enables entrepreneurs to enjoy the challenge of achieving their goals. Entrepreneurs focus on their goals because they are result-driven. For them the G.O.A.L is not ordinary! To them, G.O.A.L means:

G – **G**uarantees

O – **O**ptimal essence in

A – **A**chieving

L - **L**eadership leaps.

The goal is a commitment to protect your position and posterity, it is an assurance that empowers you to build your affluence. As a warrant that is time-specific, it commands a high level of certainty.

The optimal essence distinguishes the illusion and situates the needed drive – visualizing the output. To achieve their goals, entrepreneurs use their skills and talents, and skill being the:

S – **S**pecific

K – **K**ey

I – **I**ntended to

L – **L**ock-out

L – **L**aziness.

In using their skills, they apply their talent which is:

T – Totally

A – Able to

L – Launch

E – Elegantly

N – Normal

T – Trouble-shooting.

Talent singles you out in your need to achieve. A combination of skills and talent is enlightenment.

Skills + Talent = Enlightenment

And in using this gained enlightenment, entrepreneurs should match their talents towards sell-able (*profitable*) ideas because in the marketplace, what you need to excel is not bright ideas but sell-able ideas. And for an idea to be profitable in this fast changing business environment, the value for talents would be a premium.

Because according to William Bernbach "*An idea can turn to dust or magic, depending on the talent that rubs against it.*" You must have sell-able and profitable ideas. You have what it takes, start with your talent for talent is in the character of:

T – Trusted

A – Adaptable

L – Leverage

E – Energetic

N – Navigable

T – Turn-key.

"Everyone has talent, what is rare is the courage to follow the talent to the dark place where it leads." – Erica Jong.

An entrepreneur needs to possess the necessary skills and talents for achievement. Amar Bhidé, an entrepreneurship expert says successful entrepreneur have *"an almost maniacal level of ambition. Not just ambition to make a comfortable living, to make a few million dollars, but someone who want to leave a significant mark in the world."* Their skills and talents give them the smartness and dedication to achieve.

4. High Level of Energy

Building and running a business is energy sapping and requires long hours of work and dedication. Some entrepreneurs work full-time at their regular-day jobs and spend week-nights and weekends launching their start-ups. Many devote 14-hour days, seven days a week to their new ventures.

In his ten-year study of entrepreneurs, author Amar Bhidé found that what distinguishes successful entrepreneurs from other business owners is that they *"work harder, hustle for customers, and know that the opportunity may not last for more than six or eight months."*

One of the reasons entrepreneurs need a high level of energy is that starting a business is hard work with little or no staff and struggle to raise enough capital to stay afloat. The entrepreneur must within the limits of resources, maximize capital and practice lean management until the company stands firm. Outstanding individuals have one thing in common: absolute sense of mission. The high energy helps entrepreneurs to see opportunities when and where others don't. The entrepreneur understands that the mission is more important than anything else.

The mission is keeping an eye on the goal, it is the purpose of the organization and Purpose Achieves Destiny (*PAD*). The mission is an integral part of the organization; it examines the functions and actions of the organization, which emboldens the organization. As such organization adopt a proper mission statement.

The concept **M.I.S.I.O.N** encodes:

M – **M**ust

I – **I**nvest

S – **S**ystematically

S – **S**pecial

I – **I**nterest

O – **O**nward

N – **N**otable target.

The **M.I.S.S.I.O.N** concept specifies a target, this means that the mission is set to achieve and accomplish notable target(s). The first step in strategic thinking is to translate the organization's vision into a mission statement.

The mission statements indicate specific, achievable, inspiring principles. This is because it guides the actions of the employees, informs the customers and other stakeholders of the company's primary reason for existence. It highlights the scope of operations, the market it seeks to serve and the ways and manner of how unique the company is from that of the competitors. It is also important to note that mission statements may seem simple but their development can be one of the most complex and difficult aspects of strategic planning.

The mission statement requires detailed consideration of the organization's values and vision which forms the basis for fundamental management decisions because the mission has to be an investment of systemic special interest onward targets that are notable and can be achieved with high level of energy. The mission is the fuel that keeps the organization going and the entrepreneur must push to achieve the vision.

5. Self-Confidence & Optimism

In the words of Winston Churchill: "*A pessimist sees the difficulty in every opportunity; an optimist sees the opportunity in every difficulty.*" Entrepreneurs are optimistic individuals who have confidence in their ability to be successful based on their skills and talent. This projects a sense of fearlessness and daring actions that produce results despite any difficulty and structural hindrances.

It is said that an optimist thinks that this is the best possible world. A pessimist fears that this is true. Entrepreneurs are not immune to low and droopy spirit yet they are revived and reinvigorated because they do not give up and are constantly optimistic.

Ashish Thakkah, the founder of Mara Group is a case of self-confident and optimistic entrepreneur who started his business that is now a conglomerate (*employing over 7,000 employees with operations in 26 countries*) at the age of 15 growing up in the United Kingdom and Uganda and surviving the historic Rwandan genocide. He borrowed **$6,000** to start his first IT company. He was confident of his success that he did quit school to become a full-time entrepreneur. He was told by his parents that if the business should fail in one year he would go back to school, but he succeeded and his business is a success story.

"*Optimism is the faith that leads to achievement.*" – Hellen Keller.

6. Tolerance for Fear

Fears are those frightful things you see when you take your eyes off the goal and entrepreneurs understand this. The fears encountered by prospective entrepreneurs are fear of failure, fear of selling, fear of inadequate resources, fear of not succeeding, fear of not knowing when and how to start, fear of not testing their ideas.

Often such fears are results of indecision and lack of discipline to take the first step like a child learning how to walk but why should you have fear when you see adults walking? By now you realize there was no need to fear taking those first steps as a child, the same is applicable to business.

To conquer fears relating to starting a business, develop a mindset that is business-conscious, focus eyes and ears on what is happening in the business world, take lessons from successful entrepreneurs and be courageous. This will help in dealing with inexperience, managerial mistakes, poor location of business and poor financial control.

Entrepreneurs *"fail forward"* by taking lessons from others' experiences and seeing failure as an experience in training, otherwise, it would be termed Falling Again Into Laziness Using Ripe Errors (*F.A.I.L.U.R.E*). Entrepreneurs concur that *"It is better to fail in originality than succeed in imitation."*

In addition, fears are minimised through careful market research, feasibility study and asking questions about the industry you are interested in. Fear is a factor that prevents a lot of people from living to their full potential, but this need not be so as Maria Curie aptly puts it *"Nothing in life is to be feared, it is only to be understood."*

As such, the Sage of Omaha, Warren Buffett, the US billionaire, did say *"I will tell you how to become rich... Be fearful when others are greedy and be greedy when others are fearful."* And this has been one of his secrets to success and great wealth.

Furthermore, fear is only a distracting voice that when we close our ears to its sound it ceases to function. The answer to fear is in its name F(*EAR*). The F is fairy tales that fills the ear with distracting voices, once the ear is shut, it fades away. Moreover, as entrepreneurs it is important to avoid playing the Ostrich and to understand that fear leads to nowhere, it only keeps you in one place. A Sage once said; fear has two meanings, **F**orget **E**verything **A**nd **R**un (**FEAR**) or **F**ace **E**verything **A**nd **R**ejoice (**FEAR**). The choice is yours.

To deal with fear, entrepreneurs need to be committed to the vision for in the words of John Wolfgang Von Goethe *"Until one is committed there is hesitancy, a chance to draw back, always ineffectiveness. Concerning all acts of initiative and creation, there is one elementary truth, the ignorance of which kills countless dreams and splendid plans. That the moment one definitely commits oneself, then providence moves too."* He further stated that *"Whatever you can do or dream you can begin it. Boldness has genius, power and magic in it."* As Rich Dad noted *"a person's financial reality will not change until he or she is willing to go beyond the fears and doubt of his or her ownself imposed limits."*

Prospective entrepreneurs need not fear and take that first step or they go to the grave like the millions of talents that never started a business for fear of nothing, the grave is indeed the dumpsite of many potential people. Therefore, don't allow fear rob you of impacting the world. Start something now, it is not easy to start a business because you procrastinate just like other innovative thinkers who never get anything done.

It is necessary to move beyond the identification of opportunity to its pursuits. Steve Ross says *"You can't operate a company by fear, because the way to eliminate fear is to avoid criticism. And the way to avoid criticism is to do nothing."* Fear is a virtue of slaves.

"The free man is he who does not fear to go to the end of his thought." – Leo Blum

7. Internal Locus of Control

Entrepreneurs take personal responsibility for the success or failure of their actions. They take whatever that happens as an outcome of their actions instead of blaming someone, fate or luck. They do not make excuses because they are in control of their lives. Luck is not what entrepreneurs depend on, for it is the fools who hope in what they cannot get but dreams of; never hope in luck.

Bill Gates was once asked the role of luck on his road to success, he simply replied *"Timing and skills are the luck you have."* Do not wait on luck for everybody has got luck but you have to use your skills to get the luck for good luck is when preparation meets opportunity. It is better to be prepared for opportunities and don't have one rather than have opportunities and not be prepared.

In our daily situations, associations and activities lies in ocean of opportunities, see with your eyes, be curious with your mind, work smart, be focused, be in control and forget luck; it is the lazy man's bedfellow. Ray Kroc, the founder of McDonald's famous for its hamburger, has this to say *"Luck is a dividend of sweat, the more you sweat, the luckier you get."*

Luck is neutral, that is why there is good luck and bad luck but mainly it is a matter of adjectives and actions determine the force of luck that plays out in your pursuit. *"It is a choice decision in a subconscious stead, if not why talk of preparedness,"* we make our own luck.

In the words of Ray Kroc *"The world is filled with unsuccessful people."* Being in control aids the entrepreneurs not to loose sight of what is important, facilitate the achievement of objectives, cope with changes and take corrective actions. Having control helps to manage finances and measure performance.

8. Simplicity in Ambiguity

Albert Einstein once said *"Out of clutter, find simplicity, from discord find harmony. In the middle of difficulty lies opportunity."*

With limited funding, the typical entrepreneur cannot afford to stockpile resources to prepare for the future but must act quickly as orders come in. That was Seth Goldman's experience when he founded a company to market Honest Tea. He experimented with a variety of ingredients until he created a flavour he thought would taste good either hot or cold, then lined up an appointment with buyers at the Fresh Fields/Whole Foods chain of natural-foods grocers. He brewed his original flavour of Honest Tea in his home kitchen and took a thermos full of the tea to his appointment. The buyers were delighted and ordered 15,000 bottles. Now Goldman had a problem: he still needed a way to produce all that tea. Undaunted, he found help from an expert in the bottling industry. He arranged to have the tea produced at a factory in Buffalo. As demand for the tea grew the company diversified into eight varieties of bottled tea plus tea bags. Goldman's company purchased part ownership of a bottling facility in New Kensington, Pennsylvania.

Simplicity in Ambiguity differs from risk taking so associated with entrepreneurship. Entrepreneurs are not gamblers who risk everything because they seek for strategies that they believe have a good prospect and opportunity of succeeding.

Simplicity in ambiguity helps successful entrepreneurs deal with unexpected situations and by keeping close tab and listening to their customers adjust their services to profit from the relationship. Henry Ford, the founder of Ford Motors, says *"A handful of men have become very rich by paying attention to details that most others ignored."* We will conclude by saying that simplicity is the first order of mastery.

9. Risk Taking

Entrepreneurs are calculated risk-takers. They enjoy the excitement of a challenge, but they don't gamble. Entrepreneurs avoid low-risk situations because there is a lack of challenge and avoid high-risk situations because they want to succeed. They like achievable challenges. By accepting difficult yet achievable risks they assess their skills and apply their talents. Risk-taking is related to creativity and innovation and an essential ingredient in turning ideas into reality.

Risk is the situation that occurs when you are required to make a choice between two or more alternatives whose potential outcomes are not known and must be subjectively evaluated. A risk situation involves potential success and potential loss. The greater the possible loss, the greater the risk involved. Entrepreneurs should realize that growth comes from taking advantage of present opportunities and conditions in your personal, social and business life and making the best out of it.

Do not underestimate your own worth because as always you are able of carrying out greater things than you actually do. When you begin to see that every action you take is your own making and decision, it decreases your dependence on others because the best help you can get is the help you give to yourself, no matter how difficult it may seem at first it will soon become as always a passing phase. There is no risk until you assume control of your actions and make your own choices as you go.

Two ways to reduce risky factors are having a clear-cut awareness of your skills and talents, knowing the capacity you can control. And secondly, how you can direct challenges in your favour even using others to surmount the challenge must be in your own interest.

Entrepreneurs surmount any draw-backs and obstacles that stands in their way to success, in launching their businesses they take risks in the knowledge of the market place and available resources and still come out triumphant.

CHAPTER FOUR

RESPONSIBILITIES OF
STARTING A BUSINESS

"If you think you are too small to have an impact, try going to bed with mosquito." - Anita Roddick *(founder of the Body Shop with 2,605 shops as at 2010)*

According to Sage Vincent Ikechukwu, Business besides its simple meaning of buying and selling stands for

B – Brisk

U – Usage of

S – Securities

I – Invested in

N – Negotiable

E – Exchanges by

S – Sustained

S – Services

It is in your best interest to see through the services you provide so that you can be in business for yourself while living your entrepreneurial passion. As an entrepreneur, it is important to know that the works of your hands are blessed.

In other words, you can always prosper in business if you really want to, but you must be able to have good knowledge of your business, develop the right attitude and acquire the needed skills to do well in your business.

Just like the way it is believed that one's fingers reveal his or her personality. You have a personality as an entrepreneur! You must be able to employ your logical thinking and willpower in order to make good decisions and control your business affairs.

You must have a sense of direction and purpose that compels you to be structured and disciplined to drive your entrepreneurial passion and achieve entrepreneurial success. Let us take a look at the five fingers of the entrepreneur.

THE FIVE FINGERS OF THE ENTREPRENEUR

1. Vision

The entrepreneurs must have a vision, an idea and innovation to begin with and must keep count on it.

This helps to develop the goal, the vision and mission statements of the company. Sir Alexander Fleming, the pioneer of Penicillin said *"It is the lone worker who makes the first advance in a subject: The detail may be worked out by a team, but the prime idea due to enterprise, thought and perception of an individual."*

2. Tolerance for Fear

The entrepreneur must create and make a model that is bound to sell and adaptable to real world. He must source for information about his model. Be it a marketing strategy or an airplane. He must make a prototype for seeing is believing.

3. Network

The entrepreneur must build contacts and relationships that are profitable and relevant to his vision. He must build and have links or access to people that will pay him, for these are the people who will be his customers and also the people who will contribute to his success.

The use of the explosive and ever expanding internet and human connectivity through social media and other interwoven networks of multiple layer communities have made sharing and access to resources easier and simplified like in no other generation and this holds the power of making anyone an instant billionaire when instrumentalised for productive goals.

In building your network consistently keep in touch with persons who will help you and that you can leverage on, but in your best interest without any apology, avoid persons irrespective of their social strata; who make empty promises, persons who can help you but would not help you because such persons are unfair to you, they do not understand your purpose in life, do not value your time or loyalty and they amount to no good, including not being of any benefit to your growth network.

4. Time

The entrepreneur must be totally committed, have a sense of purpose that prevents him from the comfort of sleep and wakes him up every morning. His sense of time must realize that not everything that has beginning has continuity therefore he must have the patience for sustainability.

Time for the entrepreneur is the balancing between speed and sustainability, speed helps the value system of the venture and directs how fast the venture is bound to fare in an ever dynamic business environment while sustainability positions the venture and leads the venture in attainment of its goal through appropriate adaptations.

5. Coordination

The entrepreneur must be magnetic in linking for results. He must bring resources together and get his acts in order. He must spin his web like the spider using the 5M – Men, Materials, Money, Machines and Method.

To be magnetic means he must learn how to sell (*On how to sell, the book;* **A to Z of Selling; the Giving Strategy in business relationship by Sage Vincent Ikechukwu** *is a veritable quick reference tool and a good companion*).

ENTREPENEURIAL PITFALLS IN A START-UP

Researchers including seasoned entrepreneurs like John Osher revealed seventeen (17) commonly made mistakes by entrepreneurs and which when avoided would bring much success to the entrepreneur (*Henricks, 2004*). These mistakes are:

i. Not spending enough time researching the business ideas to ascertain its viability.

ii.   Inappropriate assessment of the market size, timing, ease of entry and potential market share.

iii.   Underestimating financial requirement and timing.

iv.   Over projection of sales volume and timing.

v.   Underestimating cost projection.

vi.   Overstaffing and spending too much on office facilities.

vii.   Lacking contingency plan for a shortfall in expected outcome.

viii. Accommodating unnecessary partners.

ix.   Hiring unnecessary hands other than sake of skills.

x.   Failing to manage the business as a whole, instead indulge in spending more time and other resources on things that are of less importance to the growth of the entire business.

xi.   Easily conceding to challenges e.g. easily accepting that "it is not possible" rather than finding a way out of it.

xii.   Having more interest and attention on sales volume and company's size rather than profit.

xiii.   Seeking approval of your action rather than going for the truth that will contribute positively to your business.

xiv.   Embarking on complex vision. This is tantamount to doing so many things at the same time and end up not doing everything right. For instance, instead of focusing energy on making sales of or improve main product, entrepreneur may be busy doing other different things that are not critical to the survival and development of the company, at the same time.

xv.   Lacking clarity of long-term aim and business purpose: Not having a clear idea of what long-term aim is detrimental to business growth.

xvi.   Inadequate focus and identity. The entrepreneur should avoid not having a clear target and identity. Going for products or services which you can't command the industry tends to give you weak identity.

xvii.   Having no exit strategy. When an entrepreneur lack exit plan it becomes difficult to know when it is proper to call it a quit by either selling the business or winding up its operations. Lack of exit plan will also affect the way the business is run. For instance, a business may enter into a contractual agreement spanning over a period longer than its winding period, thereby putting the company in unnecessary costs.

DEVELOPING BUSINESS IDEAS

Nothing kills great ideas more than people with small ideas and limited imaginations. It is said that the average person has four ideas each year, anyone of which would make them a millionaire if they would just follow it up.

In selecting an idea for your business, the two most important considerations are (*1*) finding something you love to do and are good at doing and (2) determining whether your idea can satisfy a need in the marketplace. People willingly work hard doing something they love, and the experience will bring personal fulfillment. The old adage *"Do what makes you happy"* and *"To thy own self be true"* are the best guidelines for deciding on a business idea. Warren Buffet said *"find where you have a lot of passion and energy and you will be well in whatever you do."*

Other considerations in developing business ideas may include:

1) Looking at past experiences or work done.

2) Borrowing an idea from someone's experience.

3) Being alert to trends and seeing the opportunities.

4) Government policies and regulations.

5) Franchise.

6) Hobby.

7) Self-discovery.

8) Improve on existing product.

9) Use an existing product for an untapped market.

Success also depends on customers, so would-be entrepreneurs must also be sure that the idea they choose has merit in the marketplace. The most successful entrepreneurs tend to operate in industries where a great deal of change is taking place and in which customers have difficulty pinpointing their precise needs. These industries include advanced technology and consulting, for it allows entrepreneurs to capitalize on their strengths, such as creativity, hardwork and tolerance of ambiguity to build customer relationships.

According to one study, about 3-5 percent of the companies in any industry are growing exceptionally fast, so entrepreneurs do not need to limit their insights to industry characterized by rapid growth. The study advices entrepreneurs to be not only the best but also innovative and different.

The following guidelines may help you to select an idea that represents a good entrepreneurial opportunity for you:

(i)   List your interests and abilities. Include your values and beliefs, your goals and dreams, things you like and dislike doing and your job experiences.

(ii)   Make another list of the types of business that match your interest and abilities.

(iii)   Read newspapers, business and consumer magazines to learn about demographic and economic trends that identify future needs for products that no one yet offers.

(iv)   Carefully evaluate existing goals and services, looking for ways you can improve on them.

(v)   Decide on a business that matches what you want and offers profit potential.

(vi)   Conduct marketing research to determine whether your business idea will attract enough customers to earn a profit.

(vii)   Learn as much as you can about the industry in which your new venture will operate, your merchandise or service, and your competitors. Read surveys that project growth in various industries.

Robert Allen said *"It doesn't do any good to offer customers peanuts butter if they are really hungry for honey."* This is because *"Quality in a product or service is not what the supplier puts in. It is what the customer gets out and is willing to pay for. Customers pay only for what is of use to them and what gives them value."* - Peter Drucker.

Henry Ford once said *"Anything founded on the idea of the greatest good for the greatest number will win in the end."* An entrepreneur's need for marketing research varies depending on the business idea, industry and competitive conditions. An innovative idea with an unproven potential customer base may require more research than a proposal to improve an existing product. On the internet are vast materials and resources that can help an idea into a business it all depends on how you can search and what you look for.

CHAPTER FIVE
IDENTIFICATION OF BUSINESS OPPORTUNITIES

"A business, like an automobile has to be driven in order to get results." - Bertie Charles Forbes, *founder of Forbes magazine*

E ssentially, businesses are meant to satisfy human wants, these wants are identified through market research after which products are developed and are then sold for profits.

Many businesses offer good products; but unless the entrepreneur takes advantage of market opportunities, few of these products will be sold.

Factors related to perceiving new market opportunities include conducting market research, gathering data from various sources and selecting a business location.

An aspiring entrepreneur can have an idea which he or she believes is a great idea that would be an instant success in the market. Not all such ideas can translate into viable business opportunities.

For a business idea to transform into a business

opportunity the idea must offer a viable solution to a problem experienced by potential consumers and for which they are willing to pay.

A business idea, no matter how novel, cannot be a business opportunity if customers cannot see its added value and therefore unwilling to pay for it.

Challenges create changes, it is the identification of these changes that presents the opportunities.

The following are the steps involved in analyzing business opportunities:

1) Develop the basic Business Idea: The entrepreneur should consider a product or service that has or have target customers and/or market: A business idea is a concept for a product or service that currently does not exist or is not currently available in a market niche. An idea could be a brand new concept (*radical innovation*) or an improvement to a current product or service (*incremental innovation*). A person's experience can be used to develop an idea or an idea can be generated in a moment of creative insight.

2) Scan and assess the external environment to

locate factors in the societal and task environments that pose opportunities and threats: Scanning the environment should be directed at focusing on market potential and accessibility of resources.

3) Scan and assess the internal factors relevant to the new business: The entrepreneur should consider his or her personal assets, area of expertise, abilities and experience objectively, all in terms of the organizational needs of the new venture.

4) Analyze the strategic factors in light of the current situation, using SWOT (Strengths, Weaknesses, Opportunity and Threats – The purpose of SWOT is to understand what you do well as your strengths, how you could improve on them as your opportunities, where there are adjustments to be made and what is lacking as weaknesses and the changes; how rapid or incremental these changes like Technology, unreliability of suppliers could be as your threats). The venture must be evaluated on the basis of its potential strengths and weaknesses in the light of opportunities and threats.

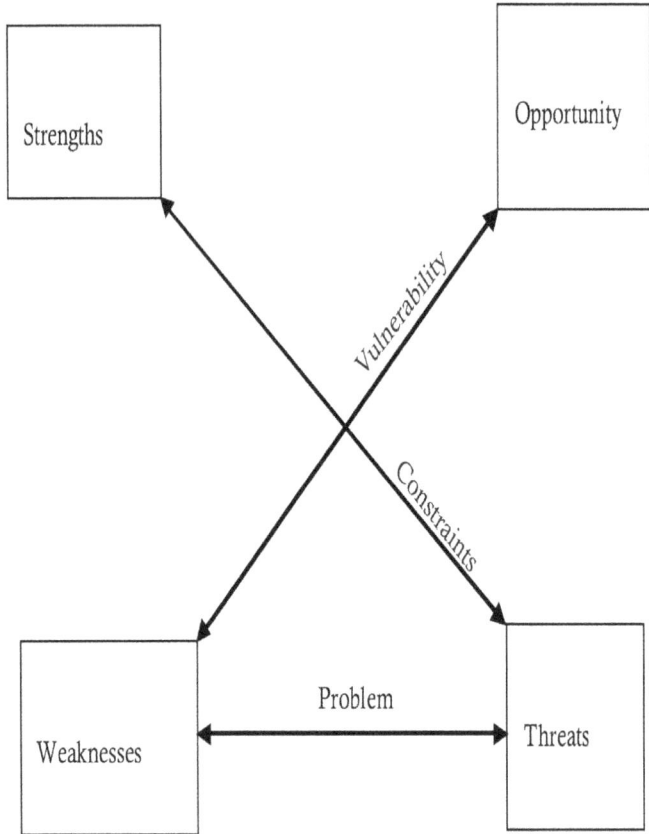

Elements of SWOT Analysis (*Adapted from Contemporary Business*)

5) Decide to go or not to go: For a business idea that appears to have a feasible business opportunity, the process should be continued. Otherwise further development of the idea should be discontinued unless the strategic factors change.

6) Generate a business plan that specifies how the

opportunity will be transformed into reality: Here, key internal factors should be specified and performance projections generated. The advantages of the business plan include financial support to be obtained from potential investors and creditors, and it increases a new venture's probability of survival and facilitates new product development. At this stage, the proposed venture's missions, objectives, strategies and policies as well as likely board of directors (*if a Corporation*) and key managers should be developed.

7) Implement the business plan: This can be done through the use of action plans and procedures.

8) Evaluate the implemented business plan through comparison of actual performance against projected performance results: To the extent that actual results are less than or much greater than the anticipated results, the entrepreneur needs to reconsider the company's current mission, objectives, strategies, policies and programmes and possibly make changes to the original business plan.

After a new business opportunity has successfully been evaluated in the idea generation stage, it should be further developed and refined through interaction with the target consumers. In the concept development stage the refined idea is tested to determine if it will be accepted to the anticipated customers.

Initial reactions to the concept can be obtained from potential customers or members of the distribution channel when appropriate. One method of measuring consumer acceptance is the conversational interview in which selected respondents are exposed to statements that reflect the physical characteristics and attributes of the product or service idea.

Favourable as well as unfavourable products or service features can easily be discovered by analyzing consumers' responses, with the favourable then incorporated into the new product or service of the selected business. Of importance in the concept development stage are questions bordering on how the new concept compares well with that of competing firms in terms of quality, reliability and validity.

Do not forget, "*In today's mercurial, unpredictable economy, businesses that fail to grow and change will stagnate and die."* - Heather Robertson. And in everything you do about your business *"Watch the cost and the profits will take care of themselves."* - Andrew Carnegie.

Therefore, profit is left to those who wish to show initiative and actually pursue rather than just think about business opportunity.

CHAPTER SIX

NAVIGATING FAILURES IN

BUSINESS

"Mistakes, risks and failures are integral part of human development." – Robert Kiyosaki *(Rich dad-Poor dad)*

Literatures abound on why businesses fail yet few offer insights on how to navigate failures in business. First and foremost, the entrepreneur must always have in mind that every organization or business is set up to offer solution(*s*) to multiplex of world problems.

As such in the words of Michael Dell, the founder of Dell computers, *"when a business goes wrong, look only to the people who are running it."* The business must continually position itself with the best hands who must see the organization as theirs and do not just be harbingers of bad news but solution providers.

The entrepreneur should with his employees ask the appropriate questions for solutions rather than buck passing, blaming others and expending the time for getting solutions on trivial issues that does not contribute to the growth of the organization. For *"it's fine to celebrate success but its important to take lessons from failure."* - Bill Gates. And remember, failures are temporary defeats which as always fade away.

Failure can be navigated by entrepreneurs through:

(1) **Being Prepared**: The Boys Scout motto is *"Be prepared."* The preparation needed must be strategic in mitigating the dire consequences of failure for entrepreneurs must look out for loopholes that lead to failures as stated earlier in the 17 Entrepreneurial pit falls in a start-up and create a workable exit strategy.

Like the athlete's 5Ps – Proper Preparation Prevents Poor Performance, entrepreneurs must know when to execute plans to be in the interest of the organization. Plans are guidelines for action, therefore must reflect changes in the business environment.

(2) **Seek for Assistance**: Assistance is having things get done from the view and hands of capable other persons. It should be professional advice from those who have the ability and capacity to tell you when you are getting it wrong and not what your ears like to hear. Oprah Winfrey said *"You have to surround yourself with people you trust and people that are good, but they also have to be people who will tell the emperor he has no clothes."*

(3) **Cooperation not Competition**: Surely every business has its fair share of competitors, they should serve as measures of strength and growth for iron sharpens iron. See your competitors as those who could help your business to be up and doing. Estee Lauder of Estee Lauder cosmetics said *"Observing your own and your competitor's successes and failures makes your inner business voice sure and vivid."* See what they your competitors are doing right then adapt to fit your own peculiar business issues.

Be wise to take lessons from your competitors and build an ethical level of cooperation for beneficial growth and also find primary areas where you can have cooperative partnership in an alliance that benefits the customer like the pooling of resources to build strong communication networks but avoid unethical cooperative partnership like price fixing and unequal arrangements that may out compete your company in the long term.

(4) **Participate in Seminars and Programmes**: There are seminars and programmes relevant to your industry. Do not just attend, participate, be open and ask questions. Even programmes that have links directly or indirectly to your industry may be the answer to your business not

failing.

(5) **Choose a Vintage Location**: The location of your business could just be the right ingredient to your business not failing. Let the environment reflect what your organization represents and not because you saw a vacant space. Factors for location should include ease of access both for your customers to reach you and for you to reach your customers, availability of labour, nearness to your market, ease of raw materials (*for industries*) and be guided by the government city or town planning regulations to avoid demolition or relocation for this can be bad for the business.

(6) **Sound Financial Control**: This is very important in avoiding failures for every business needs sound financial management, by having adequate capital and cashflow. Careless debt collection method, reckless and undisciplined spending habits lead to business failures.

(7) **Build Customer Relationship**: The entrepreneur is as good as his employees because they represent him and the business as such their attitude toward the customers matters a lot for the customer is no longer king but the dictator. Sam Walton, the founder of Walmart, said *"There is only one boss, the customer. And he*

can fire everybody in the company from the chairman down, simply by spending his money somewhere else." To be disrespectful, not tolerant in understanding customers' sensitivity and reactions, unethical practices like exploiting the customers to make fast cash, non-commitment to quality standard, leave a bad taste in the mouth of customers and makes them welcomed customers to your competitors. Remember, it is the customers that spend money not angels and your organization need the money.

In conclusion, every entrepreneur should work smartly to be able to navigate failures intelligently and seek professional and relevant help and more importantly, entrepreneurs should not be satisfied with the one and same method of doing things because in the words of Thomas Edison; *"Show me a thoroughly satisfied man, and I will show you a failure."* And if you have failed in the past do not give up, be open to innovative ideas and remember that *"failure is the opportunity to begin again, more intelligently."* – Henry Ford.

On a personal note, in business it is good to have an exit plan. Most consultants like myself do advice clients to sell or restructure the business, and as an entrepreneur, I do have an exit plan when I am going into any venture but my exit plans are guarded by my exit plan motto which I use in driving all my businesses. With respect to this, I ensure I do my feasibility study properly and also answer the hard questions before starting the business. I do this in view of the fact that I do not like the idea of winding up a business. Therefore, my exit plan motto has often been *"NO GIVING UP – KEEP INNOVATING; NO SURRENDER."*

Now you know my entrepreneurial motto, you therefore have the tool you need to keep on being innovative and not to surrender. This exit plan motto sharpens my focus on achieving my goal of being in business. I do not turn back because I must have done my homework, honestly evaluated my strategy and then determine the control measures for a profitable outcome in the exit strategy. I do my homework well and only except a successful ending, therefore I do not give up; you too can do the same.

Lastly, note that my exit plan motto is different from the actual exit strategy because the exit plan or strategy may depend on the nature of business, industry of operation and the speed of change that occurs in the business environment. This calls for being smart to know when to sell and how to negotiate the sale or in the case of restructuring, when and how to restructure the business. The phase of the business and forensic business auditing would aid the entrepreneur in the appropriate exit strategy for his or her business.

CHAPTER SEVEN
WOMEN IN BUSINESS:
OPPORTUNITIES AND
CHALLENGES

"Whatever women do they must do twice as well as men to be thought half as good. Luckily, this is not difficult"
- Dr. Charlotte Whitton *(1ˢᵗ female Mayor of Ottawa, Canada)*

The digital and fast ever changing marketplace is opening a new vista for female entrepreneurs. The number of women in business is witnessing a surge which seems as if the marketplace is the woman's natural comfort zone for growth. The woman is created to withstand stress in managing the home, the woman has been equipped to multi-task and provide for the care of the family.

According to a 2013 American Express report on the State of Women Owned Businesses, the number of women-owned firms in the United States grew *59* percent between *1997* and *2013*, one-and-a half *(1½)* times the national average. About 8.6 million women-owned businesses in the U.S are now generating more than $1.3 trillion in revenues and providing jobs for 7.8 million workers.

The Small Business Administration (*SBA*), a government agency works with many women to turn an informal business or hobby into a more formal revenue-generating enterprise. According to Wikipedia, women entrepreneurs comprise of approximately 1/3 of all entrepreneurs worldwide. The International Monetary Fund (*IMF*) recently admitted that Africa will have the fastest-growing economy of any continent over the next five years. Many of the new entrepreneurs of Africa are women.

Marcelo Giugale, the World Bank's director for poverty reduction and economic management for Africa said *"Women in private sector represent a powerful source of economic growth and opportunity."* According to World Bank data, nearly two-thirds of women are participating in Africa's labour force. The World Bank also noted that the rate of female entrepreneurship is higher in Africa than any other region of the world.

In Africa, many support-networking women entrepreneurship organizations are existing giving women the needed stand to move forward. The United

States is also supporting women entrepreneurship through African Women's Entrepreneurship Program (*AWEP*) so that women are better equipped to manage their businesses.

The typical markets in Africa are dominated by trading activities powered by women and from their sales they support their families and cater for themselves.

According UNCTAD/UNIDO, 2001 study of women entrepreneurs in some African countries (*Burkina Faso, Cote D'Ivoire, Ethiopia, Gambia, Madagascar, Mali, Morocco, Senegal, Tanzania, Zambia and Zimbabwe*) showed that more and more women are becoming self-employed and managers of micro-small and medium enterprises.

Another study carried out by USAID in Uganda revealed that 45 percent of the Small and Medium Enterprises (*SMEs*) are owned and managed by women entrepreneurs. Although, the study showed that their business activities were limited to activities such as retail of food products, used garments so on. The main characteristics of these SMEs were:

- Unregistered and mainly operating in the informal sector.

- Home based and small capital base.

- Reliance on family labour, economic activity is usually intertwined with household activities.

- Marketing and managerial functions are embryonic and undifferentiated.

- Marketing is mainly local.

These features which are characteristics of women's enterprises in Africa poses grave challenges to African women entrepreneurs; ability to harness the opportunities presented by globalization.

These challenges are not exclusive to Uganda because the formal sector activities include all those using modern methods of production; they are usually large-scale activities in the modern industries and public (*government*) sectors. The informal sector on the other hand consists mainly of small-scale units engaged in production and distribution of goods and services. They are often family owned and use labor-intensive technology.

In general, entry into the informal sector is easy; it is open to all, old and young, male and female and persons with all levels of formal education (*or none*). It includes the self-employed transport worker, trader, street-hawker, etc. In some studies, the formal sector is defined to coincide with wage employment and the informal sector with self-employment.

In Nigeria, the public (*government*) sector dominates wage employment both at state and national levels. The formal sector is usually more attractive to the educated because of its attractive wages and working conditions. In the informal sector, incentives are often low and working conditions poor. The sector is often harassed by city authorities in the name of environmental sanitation and urban beautification. Studies of informal sector activities in Nigeria show they tend to cluster in some sections of the city; the entrepreneurs had little or no education and earn low incomes.

Women tend to predominate trading activities which constitute the most common informal sector activity. Women and migrants tend to predominate in the urban informal sector. Reasons why women entrepreneurs predominate in the informal sector include the following:

- Employment in the informal sector requires minimum level of formal education which women do not possess; they are therefore compelled into self-employment in the informal sector.

- Employment in the informal sector can be easily combined with domestic responsibilities because working hours are flexible, and women can take their children to the workplace.

- Relatively little capital is required to establish a business in the informal sector.

OPPORTUNITIES FOR WOMEN ENTREPRENEURS

Globalization has created a lot of opportunities, opening up markets, access to information, expanded channels of distribution and technology. Opportunities for women as entrepreneurs in the information age and the mercurial creativity era helps improve their lot, empowers women for gender equality, raise their productivity, positions women for prestige and recognition, wealth creation and lifting families out of poverty.

Opportunities in women entrepreneurship include:

- Access to national and international markets and

to earn in hard currencies through export opportunities.

- Business growth and technical know-how through opportunities in Franchising as independent agents, licensing agreements and dealership contracting or strategic alliance.

- Access to credit and start-up funding is available to women entrepreneurs. Women entrepreneurs should seek for schemes that support their business like in Nigeria the Central Bank of Nigeria (*CBN*) in 2013 did launch 220 billion naira SMEs fund and women can tap into the funds.

- Large corporations assisting small businesses with special programmes that reserve participation of women entrepreneurs to access funds and also register as supply contractors.

- Technology acquisition and transfer is an opportunity for women entrepreneurs to gain technical know-how, acquire efficient technologies that would help in the production capacity.

- Business Support Services are open-minded to SMEs and women entrepreneurs are recognized to benefit from services like management and training programmes, consultancy services et al.

- Government policies are beginning to give opportunities to women entrepreneurs. And women entrepreneurs should avail themselves of such opportunities and programmes.

- Women business exchange programmes are beginning to gain significance and are highly encouraging so that women entrepreneurs especially in Africa reap the benefits of such programmes.

CHALLENGES OF WOMEN ENTREPRENEURS

Women entrepreneurs face challenges and they are as follows:

- High cost of doing business,

- Inadequate infrastructures.

- Access to credit facilities.

- Gender stereotyping and structural limitations.

- Family responsibilities.

- Computer literacy.

- Inadequate information on markets and financial services.

- Inadequate networks and contacts.

- Poor financial practices.

Women entrepreneurs should not be undaunted by the challenges of their job for in the words of Eleanor Roosevelt *"You gain strength, courage and confidence by every experience in which you really stop to look fear in the face. You are able to say to yourself, 'I lived through this horror. I can take the next thing that comes along.' You must do the thing you think you cannot do."* And take it from a woman entrepreneur, Anita Roddick, the founder of The Body Shop with 2,605 shops worldwide. *"Nobody talks about entrepreneurship as a survival, but that's exactly what it is and what nurtures creative thinking. Running that first shop taught me business is not financial science, it's about trading: buying and selling."*

To conclude, the National Federation of Small Businesses conducted a study that revealed that by 2018 half of all small businesses will be run by women entrepreneurs so it is a wake-up call for women to get up and be proud to be a woman entrepreneur. For Caterina Fake, the co-founder of Flickr, she said and I quote; "*So often people are working hard at the wrong thing. Working on the right thing is probably more important than working hard.*" "*There is no royal flower-strewn path to success. And if there is, I have not found it, for if I have accomplished anything in life it is because I have been willing to work hard.*" - Madam C.J. Walker, America's first female entrepreneur millionaire.

And I would like to conclude with the words of Maya Angelou when she said "*I love to see a young girl go out and grab the world by the lapels. Life's a bitch. You've got to go out and kick ass.*"

CHAPTER EIGHT
THE LAW AND ENTREPRENEURS

"In a broad sense, all law is business law because all firms are subject to the entire body of law, just as individuals are."

E ntrepreneurs operate within the environment of law and the law affects the entrepreneur.

An entrepreneur has a legal duty to safeguard the business upon establishment.

This task of business protection can become easier by using legal protections to safeguard the business.

There are many ways to protect the business, its assets and employee. One critical way is to conduct business within the most appropriate legal structure or form.

Another way is to conduct business in accordance with acceptable domestic and international legal framework.

The entrepreneur should have knowledge of the laws that impacts on his business, protects his interest and entrepreneurial activities.

The entrepreneur should be acquainted with these laws:

(1) The laws protecting entrepreneurial activities and inventions. In this case the Intellectual Property (*IP*)

(2) The laws regulating the establishment and running of business in the country of operation.

In South Africa, the South African company law regulates corporations formed under the Companies Act. In Nigeria, it is the Companies and Allied Matters Act (*1990*) and in Ghana, it is the Companies Act.

(3) The law of contract regulates commercial activities

(4) The law regulating labour and

(5) The laws promoting and protecting the rights of buyers of goods and services that is the law of Tort.

Each of these laws will be highlighted and expert advice should be sought from an attorney or consultants.

(1) Laws Protecting Entrepreneurial Activities and Inventions is the Intellectual Property (*IP*)

Common to many persons is that entrepreneurship is same thing as self-employment, this is an error for entrepreneurship is so much more than just self-employment.

As stated earlier, entrepreneurs are idea creators with a vision. They are creative people and the law recognizes their creative thinking and protects such ingenuity from piracy and other unlawful acts.

The law that protects the entrepreneur and entrepreneurial activities utilizes instruments such as patents, trade or service marks, copy rights etc.

(a) **Patents** are exclusive rights granted to an inventor or assignee for a limited period of time in exchange for the public disclosure of the invention. It is a specific technological problem, and may be a product or a process.

A patent must include one or more claims that define the invention.

These claims must meet patentability requirements such as novelty and non-obviousness with a protection timeline not less than twenty years in accordance with World Trade Organization (*WTO*) Agreement on Trade-Related Aspects of Intellectual Property Rights to prevent piracy and other unlawful acts.

Patents enable the inventor to enjoy monopoly of the rewards for the invention.

There are 3 types of patents: Design patents, utility patents and plant patents.

Countries like US, Canada, Japan and China support inventions from other countries if they are genuine, of economic and technological value.

About 95 percent of the patents granted in Canada and 40 percent of those granted in the US were to foreigners including Africans.

The US government does not provide funding for patents rather it is the government sponsored programs that do, the US Patent Trademark office can be reached through their website www.uspto.gov and counselling on patents can be accessed on the website of Boston-area Better Business Bureau (*www.bosbb.org*).

For China the Hong-Kong Special Administrative Region (*HKSAR*) can help with application and grants (*www.ipd.gov.hk*).

The caveat of patents is that it is granted by a sovereign state as such entrepreneurs should obtain patent rights from each country they want their patents to be protected.

(b) **Copy-rights** is the right given to authors, artists or creators to protect their literary, artistic or musical works over the production, distribution, display or performance of such original works.

Copyright is generated as soon as the work is fixed in a tangible form as such it may or not be filed however filing makes its easier to seek enforcement in the courts.

(c) **Trademarks** is the mark that distinguishes similar goods in the trading activities, it protects distinctive names, phrases, symbols or signs. While service marks distinguish a services from other services.

(2) **The Laws Regulating the Establishment and Running of a Business in the Country of Operation**

After the identification of business opportunities, the entrepreneur should select the appropriate legal structure for his business bearing in mind factors like the extent the owner has direct control, tax issues, the transferability of ownership and the capacity to raise capital.

The three major forms of businesses are sole proprietorship, partnership and corporation.

These forms of businesses contribute in different ways towards enhancing productivity and profitability.

Comparing The Three Major Forms of Private Ownership.

Forms of Ownership	Number of Owners	Liability	Advantages	Disadvantages
Sole Proprietorship	One owner	Unlimited personal liability for business debts	(1) Owner retains all profits (2) Easy to form and dissolve (3) Owner has flexibility	(1) Unlimited financial liability (2) Financing limitations (3) Management deficiencies (4) Lack of continuity
Partnership	Two or more owners	Personal assets of any operating partner at risk from business creditors	(1) Easy to form (2) Can benefit from complementary management skills (3) Expanded financial capacity	(1) Unlimited financial liability (2) Interpersonal conflicts (3) Lack of continuity (4) Difficult to dissolve
Corporation	Unlimited number of shareholders	Limited	(1) Limited financial liability (2) Specialized management skills (3) Expanded financial capacity (4) Economies of large scale operations	(1) Difficult and costly to form and dissolved (2) Tax disadvantages (3) Legal restriction

Source: Contemporary business

(3) **The Law of Contract Regulates Commercial Activities**

As entrepreneurs engage in their commercial and economic activities they enter into agreements which are legal and enforceable at law and a valid contract shall be deemed voluntary and of mutual assent. The law of contract protects the interests of persons entering an agreement.

(4) **The Laws Regulating Labour**: As an employer of labour, the entrepreneurs should know his own legal rights and the legal rights of his employees.

(5) **The Laws Promoting and Protecting the Rights of Buyers of Goods and Services** is the Law of Tort which is a civil wrong in common law jurisdictions. Law of tort causes legal actions for negligence and recovery of loss as damages.

The entrepreneur must know that to succeed he should avoid legal liabilities. In the words of William Ford Jr. *"There's no incompatibility between doing the right thing and making money."*

CHAPTER NINE
THE ENTERPRENEUR AND
TEAMWORK

"When a business goes wrong, look only to the people who are running it." – Michael Dell

No business can succeed under the most enthusiastic and confident entrepreneur without the full support of employees and others associated with the enterprise. The best product in the world will probably be a failure without an efficient and knowledgeable sales staff. Also, the most efficient equipment in the factory could produce unsaleable products unless competent and dedicated staff supervised and controlled it.

People and business success are synonymous. It is important for you as an entrepreneur to recognize that people represent (for your business) an investment.

Robert Winship Woodruff, the Coca-cola heir did say; *"There is no limit to what a man can do or where he can go if he does not mind who gets the credit."* For that reason, as an entrepreneur, you should be interested in people because your business success depends on them: your staff, suppliers, customers, advisers and many others.

The goal of every entrepreneur is to grow his business beyond himself. Whether an entrepreneur begins as a sole proprietor or pools resources with another to form partnership, he plans to grow the business in the future. That growth implies that he would be needing more productive resources, especially human resources and thus, the need to build collaborative teams out of his employees if he is to keep up with the mission and vision of his enterprise and remain competitive at the marketplace.

WHAT A TEAM IS

A team is a group of people with complementary skills, who are committed to a common purpose, approach and set of performance goals. All team members hold themselves mutually responsible and accountable for accomplishing their objectives. Like Michael Jordan said, *"Talent wins games but teamwork wins championships."*

Teamwork is the practice of organizing a group of workers to achieve a common objective. You have most likely experienced teamwork as a member of a sports team, debate team, band group, drama group or school project work group. Teamwork is vital in both business and other areas. The goal of a team is to increase productivity through efficient and effective actualization of set objectives.

The entrepreneur can use teams both to achieve co-ordination as part of a formal structure and to encourage employee involvement and integration. With teams, the entrepreneur builds an organisation where organizational members contribute exceptional efforts towards goal achievement; are satisfied and motivated because their initiative is being put to use; have expanded knowledge; and ensures greater organizational flexibility.

Teams are very important when it comes to achieving results and overcoming challenges that look huge to the entrepreneurs. It is therefore in the entrepreneurs' interest to maximize the right avenues and deal with the challenges. The three (3) main challenges for the entrepreneurs therefore are firstly, to build work groups into teams so as to ensure organizational effectiveness and hence, competiveness.

Secondly, the entrepreneur should be courageous and not allow fear and pride swallow up the benefits of working with and in a team if he or she really wants to grow, expand and see the business succeed. The challenge of the entrepreneur in the team would be to demonstrate coordination and a level of trust if he is to aid the team through. The entrepreneur must also be careful not to impose or overshadow a team work especially when someone else who is competent heads the team.

It is said that there is strength in numbers. This is true when this number is cohesive, united, purposive, rewarding and meaningful. The team is strength in numbers, it is a "*we*" without the "*I*" preponderance, it is about the "*us*" omitting the 'they' mentality.

The team is meant to grow organizational performance and be productive. It is this cohesive number that builds the degree of understanding. It is its unity that shows direction and focus. It is this purposiveness that enables achievement of goals. The reward of the team is its performance and the team is meaningful only when it succeeds with the aim why it was set up in the first place.

This therefore concludes that the number that makes up a team should be in the first place proportionately adequate and manageable (*A team size should range between 4 – 20 members depending on scope, function, and management.*) Ray Oglethorpe of AOL Time Warner believes the ideal size is fewer than 10 members. Ideally, your team should have 7 to 9 people. If you have more than 15 or 20, you're dead: the connections between team members are too hard to make. As a general rule, a team of more than 20 members should be divided into sub teams, each with its own members and goals.

For a team to achieve its purpose and increase productivity it should imbibe GROW. This growth is significant because it coordinates the team's effectiveness. The GROW significance of a team is

G – **G**oal commitment.

R – **R**ole Specification.

O – **O**rganized Interdependence.

W – **W**ork Appreciation.

GOAL COMMITMENT

The primary aim for having the team must be communicated and commitment by all members should be pursued, any dissenting member should be replaced with another person of equal competence who would be committed or else the dissenting member may corrupt other members towards the goal and derail focus. When there is goal commitment by all it increases the power of the team to complete the task on time and reduces energy dissipation.

ROLE SPECIFICATION

When each member knows that he or she has a special role to play and the specified role is critical to the overall success, there exists that zeal to see that their roles do not suffer and also increases participative satisfaction. Role specification enables acceptance of the role being carried out by each member and positions for unity in diversity among team members. This is true since there is the understanding that every member has something to contribute in the team, this particularly provides a linking synergy on performance and what the team expectation is.

ORGANIZED INTERDEPENDENCE

Organized interdependence shows the degree of support among members, strengthens relationship, covers for inherent weaknesses and diversity. It brings balance into the team. Like they say in the battle field *"when you are in the war front you don't fight for the barracks you fight for the man next to you, so that you can survive."* In this case, the next man is your back eye and you are his and you both look out for one another. It means every member is responsible in part for each other's success. This requires a high level of trust and deepened interaction among teammates.

WORK APPRECIATION

This provides measures of ongoing commitment through feedback support systems, evaluative improvement and acknowledging the team's success with congratulatory incentives, this further encourages standards of performance. It is also important to recognize specific individual contribution rather than praise the individual, which is a more effective approach in teamwork appreciation.

TEAMWORK

Earlier, we said that teamwork is the practice of organizing a group of workers to achieve a common objective. Teamwork is the collaborative effort utilized to plan, approach and execute a task. Teamwork is useful because it makes the task easier.

Teamwork is an important consideration in employee recruitment and training, because it encourages employees to pool their talent and ideas as individuals.

It also develops a positive social-emotional bonding among staff and provides a support post in productivity and benefits the entrepreneur. For a team to work productively and succeed in its objective, it should adopt a teamwork strategy which is:

T – **T**ask on the skills and knowledge required.

E – **E**nrich with useful tools, and socio-emotional

bonding.

A – **A**nticipate situations that may amend the objective.

M – **M**eet obstacles head on and stop bickering.

W – **W**hat actions to be taken, by whom should be

understood.

O – **O**utline the measures of commitment and

compensation.

R – **R**einforce the GROW significance.

K – **K**eep your eyes on the objective.

The concept of teamwork also applies to entrepreneurs. The key to success in managing the growth of a new venture often rests with the founder's ability to assemble a team of employees who bring complementary skills and experiences to his or her own. Perhaps, the greatest challenge for an entrepreneur who wants to encourage teamwork is to sit back and let the team generate ideas.

STAGES OF TEAM DEVELOPMENT

Teams can increase productivity, raise morale and nurture innovation. However, these benefits result only if the type of team created matches the task to be accomplished. In addition to matching the type of team to the task, managers must select the right types of people to become team members. Although many firms use teams, they often limit participation to certain groups of employees.

According to management author, Richard Daft, teams typically go through five stages of development:

1. Forming

2. Storming

3. Norming

4. Performing

5. Adjourning

We will attempt to adapt a summary of these five stages of team development as proposed by Boone and Kurtz in their book *Contemporary Business*.

1. **Forming**: this stage is an orientation period during which team members get to know each other and find out what is permitted and acceptable to the group. Team members begin with curiosity about expectations of them and if they would fit in. Time for acquaintance and getting to know each other is necessary if they are going to be socio-emotional bonding.

2. **Storming**: the personalities of team members begin to emerge at this stage as members clarify their roles and expectations. Conflicts may arise as members disagree over team's mission and hustle for position and control of the team. Subgroups may form based on common interests or concerns. At this stage team leader must encourage everyone to participate, allowing members work through their uncertainties and conflicts. Teams must move beyond this stage to

achieve real productivity.

3. **Norming**: at this stage, it is expected that members have resolved their difference, accept each other and reach a consensus about roles of the team leader and other participants. This stage is usually brief in duration, and the team leader should use it to emphasize the team's unity and the importance of its objectives.

4. **Performing**: team members focus on solving problems and accomplishing tasks at this stage. They interact frequently and handle conflicts constructively from all members and facilitate task accomplishment. High cooperation is required at this stage.

5. **Adjourning**: the team disbands at the adjourning stage after member have completed their assigned task or solved a problem. During this phase, the focus is on wrapping up and summarizing the team's accomplishments. The team leader may recognize the team's accomplishments with a celebration, perhaps handing out plaques or awards.

Furthermore, Boone and Kurtz set out a 9 step–by-step

approach to forming effective teams. They are as follows:

Step 1	Study other companies' teams.
Step 2	Involve appropriate people in planning and implementation teams.
Step 3	Seek and encourage feedback from team members.
Step 4	Set realistic goals and distribute schedules.
Step 5	Be prepared to slow down when necessary.
Step 6	Regularly evaluate and adjust the original plan.
Step 7	keep all tem members informed.
Step 8	Be prepared to resolve conflict and confusion.
Step 9	Prepare a plan for team members' compensation.

These steps should aid the entrepreneur in forming a team that is effective and the importance of having a team is exemplified by the Nigerian proverb which says *"If you want to go fast, you go alone but if you want to go far, you take other people with you."*

CHAPTER TEN

DO-IT-YOURSELF (*DIY*): BUSINESS PLAN MADE SIMPLE

"In order to be successful, you must do what others won't do, so that you earn that success others won't." - Les Brown

"There is no scarcity of opportunity to make a living at what you love to do, there's only scarcity of resolve to make it happen." - Wayne Dyer

Plans give the organisation a sense of purpose and focus, hence the plans of the business should be well written and documented. For business plan provides an orderly statement of a company's goals, the method by which it intends to achieve these goals and the standards to measure its achievements. The goals of the business must be clear, for a **G.O.A.L** as previously stated:

G – **G**uarantees

O – **O**ptimal essence in

A -**A**chieving

L – **L**eadership leaps.

The entrepreneur should answer these questions before commencing with the business plan:

- How would you explain your idea to a friend?

- What purpose would the business serve?

- Does your idea differ from existing business?

- What is the state of the industry you are entering?

- Who will be your customers? How will you market your goods and services?

- How will you finance your business?

- What characteristics qualify you to run this business?

- How will you measure your firm's success or failure at specific time intervals?

- Does the name of your proposed business reflect what you do and your firm's goals?

- Is it already registered by someone else?

- Is it offensive to any religious or ethnic group?

It is imperative that you do your research very well and waste no time in committing the business plan to paper for in the words of William Jennings Bryan *"Destiny is not a matter of chance, it is a matter of choice, it is not a thing to be waited for, it is a thing to be achieved."*

A business plan can help in achievement evaluations and help investors understand you and your business. It need not be such a hassle since there is no universal structure it must strictly follow. A business plan should be well structured to cover important areas of the business activities and indicate whether the business would be organized as a sole proprietorship, partnership or corporation. It should also identify when it will need to hire employees, job description for employees, lines of authority in the business, risk management plan, detailed information on insurance, a list of supplies with methods of assessing their reliability and competence, etc.

Since the business plan is an essential tool for securing funds the financial projections, it requires detailed information. If certain assumptions underlie the body of the plan, tie them into the financial plan. A plan for two outlets, for example, should provide cash-flow projections that show how the firm will cover the cost involved with each. Deal with significant and insignificant variables as carelessness with seemingly insignificant variables can undercut credibility. The assembled plan should be neat and easy to use. It should include a table of content so that readers can turn directly to the parts that most interest them. Also, the format should be attractive and professional. This template will guide you in crafting a good business plan.

(1) **EXECUTIVE SUMMARY**: Write down a summary of your business plan, the nature of business, its kind of products or services, why it is special, who will be managing it, how much cash you will need, when you will use it and what you will be using it for. The executive summary shall answer the who, what, why, when, where and how of your business in brief. Although the summary appears early in the plan, it probably should be the last element written.

(2) **INTRODUCTION**: This is the business overview describing your business what you want to achieve and the necessary measures to carryout your plan. It should include your vision statement, mission statement, corporate values, like customer service, the goal of your business actions, the objectives you have set for your business. Mention how much cash you will need to start or expand the business, how you will generate revenue

for the business usually in percentages to total revenue. Assess the revenues to the industry's total revenue to know your market share and your market growth prospects which is to identify opportunities and possible competitive forces and how they affect your financial projections. It should also include a brief description of your education, skills, experiences and training with references to a resume included later in the plan.

(3) **ORGANIZATIONAL STRUCTURE**: This explains the type of organization whether it is a manufacturing or service based company. Mention if your firm is incorporated, the type of incorporation and the major stakeholders of the business like the suppliers etc.

(4) **INDUSTRY ANALYSIS**: This should examine as well as explain how well you know the industry you are or wanting to operate in. Describe the industry, who the competitors are, if the industry is dominated by few big players, does the industry experience quick technological changes and how does it affect the product(s) or services. Mention the role of pricing in the industry, if the industry has an untapped market for growth, does consumer tastes change frequently and

how your business can be affected by these. Describe if there are substitutes for your product(s) or services, barriers to be faced, what the powers of distributors and suppliers are and that of consumers. Explain the cost variable in the industry, what your revenue would be and the profit margins.

Using the SWOT Analysis, describe your business strengths in terms of innovative product, patents and location of the business. The weaknesses in reference to items like high cost or disadvantage in business location, unreliable suppliers. On opportunities, describe if new technologies would give you an opportunity to grow and how they can impart on the overall business. And mention the threats like the entrance of new competitors, government regulations and threats that can reduce your profitability.

(4b) **PRODUCT/SERVICE ANALYSIS**: Describe the product(s) or service that you are bringing to the marketplace. Is the products or services already in the market or at the research and development (*R&D*) stage? Explain how you would launch the product or services and the timeframe for the launch. Mention what makes the product or service unique, at what cost you are selling, how it can compete and the profit margin. Observe that your product answers these questions:

- Is there a need for it?

- What solutions does your product solve?

- Does the product answer the customer questions?

(5) **MARKET PLAN**: This is a review and analysis of your product or service and of the competitors by distinguishing your primary target market, the size of your market by spatial location with an estimate of the population in the location. Describe your market share in percentages and the number of customers you do estimate to own in the targeted market. Do not forget to state the method used to develop the estimates.

You should also include who buys your product(s) or services, what they buy, why they buy, where they do buy, when they buy while defining the target market. You also have to analyze your closest competitors in the same chain of business, how profitable they are, where they are located, how long they have been operating the business, and what is their selling advantage or strategy.

State the ways your competitors' business is superior or inferior to your business, what percentage of market-share they currently enjoy, whether their business is experiencing growth or not and why. Describe the similarities or differences between your business operations and that of your close competitors, the sections your competitors have an upper hand over your business and how you would tackle such.

State what your business pricing objectives are and if your price is higher or lower. It should also point out any unique or distinctive features of the business including industry cycles such as busy and slow seasons and explain the reasons for choosing a particular start-up date. This should also cover equipment rentals, leasing or purchase cost and the influence of traffic volume, neighbouring business, demographics, accessibility and visibility. Further discussion should review labour cost, utility access rates, police and fire protection, zoning restrictions and government policies and regulations.

(5b) **MARKETING SYSTEM**: In this section you have to explain your pricing strategies, stating how you can use the pricing to achieve gross profit margin with items like cash discount, bulk discount etc. Outline the media you would employ to advertise so as to reach your target market, the purchasing power of your target market and how often they buy with supporting data. Here you would also have to give detailed benefits and features of your product(s) or services in terms of functionality, appearance, quality and intrinsic values. Does your business have any promotional plan in order to achieve its marketing objectives? You have to state it clearly.

(5c) **SALES STRATEGY**: This deals with how do you sell your products or services; direct sales, through mail, in stores, with sales representatives or consultative selling. What distribution channel would be employed, how fast can you produce and how much stock of the product can you store. How can you manage high or low demands? Explain how you would motivate your sales force, are your sales persons going to be temporal or permanent or both. Lastly, you would have to identify and analyze your sales pushing and/or pulling promotional strategy.

(6) **FINANCIAL PLAN**: Many investors are interested in the financial projections. If you do not have financial background you might at this stage seek the help of an expert because it entails income statements, your

revenues, expenses and profit calculations for a time period of say three to four years proposition and indices. It should detail operating plan forecast, estimates of assets and liability, analysis showing when the business would reach the break-even point – the level of sales at which revenues equal cost also a description of plans for spending funds.

(6b) CURRICULUM VITAE (CV) OF PRINCIPALS: The CV of principals should be included in a plan written to obtain funding.

Now you have the tools to write a professional business plan. You can also use business plan softwares that are available. These softwares would help, therefore there should be no delay in starting to write one now. Just get on with it, it is worth the effort. The Chinese proverb says *"He who deliberates fully before taking a step will spend his entire life on one leg."* This is supported by Cardinal Newman that *"A man would do nothing if he waited until he could do so well that no one would find fault with what he has to do."* I will conclude that innovators see things of the past; and say *"why not innovate."* Thinkers see things of the future; say *"when that time comes..."* Creators see things of the future; and say *"let us make it"* Others hear things of the future and say *"Never can it be possible."* Which one are you? Bear in mind that the spirit of the past and the future is in the present; and the present is a gift use it well.

The 6WH1 of a selling business plan: A business plan that would sell in the eyes of investors must answer these questions in a clear and concise approach for the busy investor looks at:

- Who are you?

- What are you selling?

- Why are you selling?

- How do you sell?

- Whom do you sell to?

- Where do you sell?

- When do you sell?

CHAPTER ELEVEN

FINANCING THE BUSINESS

"Banks will lend you money if you can prove you don't need it" - Mark Twain. And so, when you are preparing to borrow for investments bear in mind that *'If you owe ten pounds to the Bank of England, you get thrown in jail, but if you owe a million pounds, they invite you to sit on the Board."*

- Philippe Ries

We earlier defined business to mean

B - Brisk

U - Usage of

S - Securities

I - Invested in

N - Negotiable

E - Exchange by

S - Sustained

S - Services.

The brisk usage of securities is important in how we manage, control and utilize the business securities such as money. All business activity revolves around money (*capital*). When more money flows into a business than out of it, there will be profits. Knowing how to be entrepreneurial in managing your financial affairs is essential to being profitable in business.

As an entrepreneur you want to succeed; you want to be in control of your day-to-day financial affairs; you want to know that the future is being looked at carefully, with plans for uncertainties; and that prospects continue to meet your objectives. One item that keeps turning people off when talking of starting a business is *"I have no enough money to start," "where do I get the money to start."*

The fear of not having enough money to carryout projects has limited many would-be entrepreneurs but this ought not to be because the entrepreneurs takes risk with the limited money to build what attracts and magnets the capital needed. From my findings most would-be entrepreneurs think that money is all it takes to do business. They believe that once you get the cash to start, the business can succeed but this is not the case. A look at some companies especially the Dot.com companies that had funding of above 50 million dollars and failed to succeed separates the reality from financial myths. Sound financial planning and managerial control are strong factors to succeed including ability to manage changes and innovate are critical to the entrepreneur's success. Examples of Dot.com companies that had the money but failed:

(i) Pets.com, an online pet supply store that raised $82.5 million in IPO (*even Amazon.com acquired 40 percent shares and pressured investment banks not to underwrite the offerings of competing online pets supply companies*) failed just after nine (9) months.

(ii) Kozmo.com, an online store and delivery services raised $280 million and secured $150 million in promotion deal with Starbucks also failed.

(iii) Go.com a destination site funded by Disney went down with $790 million. Now Go.com, only acts as a referral site for Disney as it is no longer profitable.

The lesson is no successful entrepreneur had gone into business without consulting the market.

"*The market will pay to entertain than educate.*" – Warren Buffet.

This explains that capital is good but not the only need

of a business, taking this lesson in mind, let us go into financing proper. A key issue in any business plan is financing. How much money will you need to start your business and where will you get it? Capital is the money an entrepreneur needs to start the business. The nature of the business, the type of facilities and equipments will determine the capital needed.

Recent development indicates that access to capital continues to be the most difficult challenge for new ventures and small business owners. There are several reasons while, even under optimal conditions, entrepreneurs are still not successful at getting adequate funding. Banks by the very nature of their business, are resistant to the high-risk loans, which loans given to many small businesses represent. Potential entrepreneurs may also lack the business know-how to articulate what they need in business terminology.

SOURCES OF FUNDING

- Personal savings, personal credit cards and personal assets.

- Family and friends.

- Trade Credits and Accruals.

- Business credit cards and line of credit.

- Car and mortgage loans.

- Equipment loan, financial lease and high purchase.

- Commercial Bank loan and financial institutions.

- Equity financing and stock option.

- Venture capitalists.

- Angel investors and money lenders.

- Rotating savings scheme.

- Debentures (*loan stock*).

- Capital markets.

- Crowd funding and Hamrabee.

- Partnership funding.

- Retained earnings (*ploughed back investment*).

Jim Rohn said "*Part of your heritage in the society is the opportunity to become financially independent*" in good support of what Woody Allen did say that "*money is better than poverty, if only for financial reasons.*" At this juncture, it is appropriate to explain the above list of sourcing for funding for a business venture. Entrepreneurs can exploit more than one source to shore up their cashflow according to need and strategic importance.

(1) Personal Savings, Personal Credit cards and Personal Assets:

(a) Personal Savings: Most investors will not commit their capital into any venture without conscious commitment from the entrepreneur by way of proof and believe in the success of the venture. Personal savings help entrepreneurs make the first commitment and support the goal of the business.

Entrepreneurs can deliberately put aside a certain amount of cash as savings to start or execute a project, this amount of savings can come from amount saved from certain abstinence like calculating the cash you would have use to smoke or take alcohol and saving it for your venture, little by little it would become significant.

Another way of personal savings is abstaining from unnecessary and impulsive buying for example, I needed cash for a certain project and gave a ceiling to the amount of recharge I would expend on my phone credit each week and also controlled my communication expense by only making necessary calls and at the end of a year, had enough to execute two different projects.

Another way of personal savings is for women to have their own gardens no matter how small, then have a piggy bank where the money that is meant for such items like pepper, tomatoes, onions, vegetables are saved and the end of a year you will discover you have some tangible amount saved including the surplus cash from other savings sources.

(b) **Personal Credit Cards**: For those who use credit cards, this is a good source to kick-start that venture you have been putting off. Personal credit cards are usually provided by financial institutions and you can have more than one personal credit card to maximize the effect of *"pooling together."* Sandy Lerner used personal credit cards to start Cisco Systems. Ask your banks of personal credit cards facilities available to you and start your business now. It is a short term loan option with regular monthly repayment plan.

(c) **Personal Assets**: Funds can be raised by selling your personal items and effects such as phones, vehicles, landed property, jewellery, etc, it is an easy way to raise cash. In the flea market (*second hand goods*) for example, sites like nextworth.com, Usell.com, Gazelle.com deals with used gadgets and the prices are competitive and black-markets are available to resell your personal assets and gain the much needed seed capital.

"Pay now, play later; play now, pay later." - John C. Maxwell.

(2) **Family and Friends**: This is a convenient source of funding a venture. Loans or investments from this source should be a businesslike arrangement to avoid problems and do not fail to repay as arranged and keep it strictly business. However, due to present economic challenges or sheer malice some family members are not willing to assist, so to surmount such disappointment seek for only those who are willing not those who can as well as be convincing in your request because they may not see you as serious for whatever reason. Be businesslike in your approach and see them as investors not only as family and friends.

(3) **Trade Credits and Accruals**

(a) **Trade Credits:** A Trade credit is a purchasing

agreement for goods and equipments from a supplier who finances the purchase and you pay for them at a later date. This often requires that a business have good credit history of repayment. This is called purchase on account and represents the target source of short-term financing for companies. It is an unsecured form of financing since no specific assets are pledged as collateral for the liability. If the trade credit is for an intangible goods or services, it is called an *"accrual."*

(b) **Accruals** are carry-over or roll-over for goods and services that have been received or supplied but have not been paid for over a period of time. This largely depends on the entrepreneur's standing before the creditor's perception.

(4) **Business Credit Cards and line of Credit**

(a) **Business Credit Cards:** This is available to business accounts who can access credits on their accounts just like the personal credit cards. It allows the card holder to pay for goods and services based on the holder's promise to pay for them, it gives the cardholders cash advance allowing a continuing balance of debt, subject to interest being charged. Business credit cards like personal credit cards typically involve a third-party entity (*the credit card companies and financial service providers*) that pays the seller or supplier and is reimbursed by the cardholder.

(b) **Line of credit** is an agreement between a bank and a borrower indicating the maximum amount of credit the bank will extend to the borrower. It is always good to establish a credit line with your bank before you need it. This may take different forms like overdraft, export credit. Interest is usually paid only on actual money withdrawn and can be or not be secured by collateral.

(5) **Car and Mortgage loans**: This is also a good source for business financing. They expand the avenues an entrepreneur can access loans and grow the business.

(6) **Equipment loan, financial lease and hire purchase**

(a) **Equipment loan**: This provides for loans to procure equipments like Tractors and other costly equipments needed for the business success. Some businesses prefer to lease equipment rather than loan them, this might be economical for start-ups to lease but the long term consideration may make loans a worthy option.

(b) **Finance lease** is the form of acquiring an equipment for use for a period of time by paying for the time the equipment would be in use without owning the equipment. The asset does not belong to the lessee for there is no intention to transfer ownership of title to the user of the asset.

(c) **Hire Purchase** is the credit sale agreement that allow the hirer or purchaser to gain full ownership of the asset on completion of the total payment of the goods hired. The hirer or purchaser pays the hire purchase instalments over an agreed period giving the entrepreneur financial liquidity for other projects.

(7) **Commercial banks and Financial institutions**: These are formal institutions who provide financial services to lend a specific sum of money for a specific period of time. The banks usually consider these factors before granting loans:

i. The purpose of the loan.

ii. The amount involved.

iii. The duration of the loan.

iv. The financial history of the borrower.

v. The security or collateral of the loan.

(8) **Equity Financing and stock option**

(a) **Equity Financing:** Entrepreneurs invest their own money along with funds supplied by other people and firms that become co-owners of the start-ups. Incorporated companies can raise capital through the sale of stock or equity to investors who are willing to invest on long-term basis and become part owners of the firm. Equity financing can be from friends, relatives, business partners, venture capitalists and private owners.

(b) **Stock Option**: is another source of financing open to entrepreneurs by giving ownership stakes in the company in return for the financing money. Stock options can also be applied to retaining employees under Employee Stock Ownership Plan (*ESOP*) for employees to work harder and smarter and help grow the firm by attracting and keeping talented employees.

(9) **Venture Capitalists**: A venture capital company can provide capital in exchange for equity in the venture. Venture capitalists engage in financing new small business with good prospects of Return On Investments (*ROI*). They often rely on the business plan to decide either to invest or not. Arthur Rock, the venture

capitalist who helped establish Intel (*the world producer of microprocessor for computers*) with $2.5 million said "*I mean I wasn't a founder in the sense that I contributed anything scientifically but in the sense that I signed the corporation papers and, owned founder's stock.*" This clearly tells you how the venture capitalist works, they look for the business idea; financing plans, break-even analysis, projected monthly and yearly income statements; financial ratio analysis; demand for the product analysis; market research and plan for the product or service, legal structure, the profit and loss account and balance sheet, competitive advantage; management; start-up and operating costs. The client must provide all this information in the executive summary of the business plan.

(10) Angel Investors and Money Lenders

(a) **Angel Investors:** Angel investors consists a larger source of investors in start-ups. They are willing wealthy individuals who invest in new ventures for equity stakes. They invest more capital in start-ups than venture capitalists. They provide cash and expertise for equity because they are also entrepreneurs who are successful and know the difficulties of launching a business.

(b) **Money lenders** are lenders who borrow from financial institutions and re-lend to others at higher interest rates and within a short period of time for repayment, therefore they should be a last resort source for funding.

(11) **Revolving Savings System (RSS)** are informal institutions that members organize themselves to contribute a certain amount of money from which members take the accumulated funds in turns. It works this way, a group of 10 or 12 persons may organize themselves to contribute $100 each month, then each month total collection is given to a member who utilizes the money for his or her personal project and each member take their turn till it starts all over again, members choose months that are favourable to the timing of their project.

In this case, a collection of $100 monthly for 12 persons will amount to $1,200 for each member per month. Many African communities practice this and the main beneficiaries are the market women who participate in it.

Entrepreneurs can benefit from such RSS. Another variant of this system is the practice of members contributing all year round, what is accumulated is then shared at the end of the year usually in November or December based on personal contribution capacity.

(12) **Debentures (*Loan Stock*)**: It is the written acknowledgement of a debt incurred by a company containing provisions as to the payment of interest and eventual repayment of principal. This is a long-term debt finance raised by a company for which interest is paid usually at a fixed rate.

(13) **Capital Markets**: You can obtain funds for expansion from the capital market by incorporating your company and having your company listed on the Stock Exchange. Once listed you can raise funds by offering your shares for sale.

(14) **Crowd Funding and Harambee**

(a) **Crowd Funding:** Crowd funding is a novel source of funding a business or project. According to Wikipedia, crowd funding or crowd-sourced funding is the collective effort of individuals who network and pool their money via the internet to support efforts initiated by other people or organizations. As of 2012 there were over 450 crowd funding platforms. Examples of crowd funding sites are: Crowdcube.com, Seedrs.com,

Kickstarter.com, Microventures.com, Fundageek.com.

(b) **Harambee**: This is a practice majorly in Kenya, East Africa for self help community projects. Although it is an African practice and can be found in many cultures, the word itself is of East African meaning Community Self-help, in Swahili, the word means *"all pull together"* providing manual labour to undertake a project like building a house or raising a barn. For the entrepreneur, this can be adopted in his/her venture by seeking the help of his network to provide service he or she would not be able to pay for directly. Sometimes in exchange for his or her own service in the network.

(15) **Partnership Funding**: The entrepreneur can raise funds through partnership with another person who can fund the business as a silent or inactive partner. This source of funding can bring in conflicts about ownership but a partnership deed should be properly drawn to reduce conflicts.

(16) **Retained Earning (*Ploughed-back Investments*)**: This is usually for established firms looking for money for growth or expansion. It means ploughing back the profits as reinvestment in the business. To effectively use this no purchase is to be made if it is not justified in an

increase in sales and reinvest the sales profit to grow the business. Entrepreneurs can maximize this approach instead of taking a loan.

The range of finance available is surprisingly wide, and the costs and conditions vary from one type of fund to another. It is important for the entrepreneur to consider all alternatives, seek professional advice and determine the mix of finance that maximizes the potential for the business enterprise. I tell people that it is in borrowing that we process riches; not through dire savings, for all rich-men borrow including governments and they do it in a certain way. This position is affirmed by Wallace Wattles when he said *"Getting rich is not a result of savings or thrift."*

THE STAGES OF NEW VENTURE DEVELOPMENT AND FINANCING

"A corporation is a living organism; it has to continue to shed its skin. Methods have to change. Focus has to change. Values have to change. The sum total of those changes is transformation." – Andrew Grove.

Hence the entrepreneur needs to understand that money and ideas come together to provide benefits. Financing a venture traditionally takes six stages and the business at each stage needs a different type of financing, a good knowledge of these stages would help position the venture for marketplace leadership.

According to Arkebaur (*2008*) as quoted in Entrepreneurship: A practical Approach (*2008*). The six stages are:

1. Seed or Concept Stage

2. Start-up

3. First State

4. Second State

5. Maturity Stage

6. Decline Stage

These would be described briefly with sub-themes as status, tasks and financing.

1. SEED OR CONCEPT OR INCEPTION

STATUS: This is the wild-eyed, perhaps incurable inventor stage. There is an idea, a concept, but no management team. Business plan, time table and market research have not been assembled.

TASKS: To begin development of a prototype business plan and assemble some key management team.

FINANCING: The risk level of this stage is too high, hence traditional venture capitalists and other external financiers have no interest in funding this venture. It is only personal savings or friends and family money that can fund this stage.

2. START-UP OR EARLY GROWTH

STATUS: At least one principal person of the company is pursuing the venture on a full-time basis. The business plan is being refined and prototype is being developed, market analysis is being undertaken and initial customers identified.

TASKS: Complete and test the prototype to obtain evidence of commercial interest. Assemble and identify initial management team, finish the business and marketing plans, establish manufacturing and initial sales.

FINANCING: Bank overdrafts, trade credits, hire purchase and leasing are potential funding sources at this stage. Traditional venture capital firms may show interest if top rated management team is assembled, patentability or proprietorship is proven, and marketability is demonstrated.

3. FIRST STAGE OR RAPID GROWTH STAGE

STATUS: The venture is now a going concern. The product has been proved manufacturable and is selling. The initial management team is in place, the company has experienced some setbacks, customers can confirm product or service usage, marketing is being refined, adjustments are being made in the business plan and money raising efforts can continue.

TASKS: To achieve market penetration and initial sales goals, reach close to break-even, increase productivity, reduce unit costs, build sales organization and distribution system.

FINANCING: At this stage, traditional venture capital firms are interested; in fact, it is their most preferable stage. Other long term institutional finances are also introduced into the venture.

4. SECOND STATE OR DEVELOPMENT GROWTH STAGE

STATUS: Significant sales are developing so also are the assets and liabilities. The company is sporadically achieving break-even and cash flow management becomes critical.

TASK: To obtain consistent profitability, add significant sales and back orders, expand sales from regional to national level and obtain working capital to expand marketing, accounts receivable and inventory.

FINANCING: More sophisticated and second round venture capital financing comes into play. Dilution of ownership and control is also obtained through equity or stock financing.

5. MATURITY STAGE

STATUS: All systems are really good and the potential for a major success is beginning to be apparent. Unexpected or hidden difficulties are being worked out in all areas from design and development of second generation products, to marketing and distribution.

TASKS: To increase market reliability and maintain return on investment and begin to dress up the company for harvest.

FINANCING: Long-term debt financing such as debentures and other forms of external institutional financing are applied at this stage to carry increased accounts receivable and inventory prior to harvest.

6. DECLINE STAGE

STATUS: There is declined return on investment; the end may be near for the entrepreneurial companies because what started as a dream has become a reality.

TASKS: Sifting and sorting out different available options to ensure probable survival of the firm.

FINANCING: Going public, acquisition, selling-out, take-over, mergers and liquidation are the financing options at this stage. The next challenge is to start all over again, but this time with cogent experience and pocket full of cash.

CONCLUSION

FINAL THOUGHT

"If there is hope in the future, there is power in the present."
- John C. Maxwell

Believing you have read this book from the beginning to this stage, you have successfully followed your curious mind to see and know the end of this entrepreneurial expedition.

Now is the time to make the decision and take action by identifying who you are and what you can do. And when you have identified your entrepreneurial calling, go out and present your answer of the two above questioning to the first person you would meet outside your home as this would be your first marketing gig and act as a necessary push to follow through in what you can do.

The entrepreneurial journey is not a promise of all is easy, for you must bear in mind that it is the little bolts and nuts of trial and error that builds the big engine of success. Know this for sure, you cannot triumph without trying therefore go out and achieve for the Latin maxim says *"Providence assists not the idle."* And do keep in mind that it is not easy to start a big business but it's easy to start from somewhere no matter how little, just start! This is because Irving Washington said *"Great minds have purposes; little minds have wishes."*

Furthermore, do not just pass through this life and be lost in history, be a history breaker by achieving something worthwhile for history is made by individuals, who make meaningful impact in life. It is convincing to say that history is primarily the story of successful individuals, and it is no brainbox that it is called His-(s)tory.

Therefore, do bear in mind that your history cannot change if you do not take charge of the decisions that determine that future you so desire.

"Change will not come if we wait for some other person or some other time. We are the ones we have been waiting for. We are the change that we seek." - President, Barrack Obama, United States First African-American President.

Therefore, I humbly say thank you for making me your guide by reading this inspired writing. From here-upon your entrepreneurial journey has begun, and so go ahead and take action for it is your destiny to make history and you have my prayers, my love and support for success. Always have in mind that, *"Being an entrepreneur is about having the will and determination and not being frightened of getting it wrong."*

REFERENCES

Boone L.E and Kurtz D.L (2002) *Contemporary Business*, tenth Ed. Harcourt College Publishers, USA.

Geofrey G.M; Robert E.N; Philip A.N (1986) *The Practice of Entrepreneurship*, University of Lagos Press, Nigeria.

McOliver F.O; Okafor F.C; Nwagwu N.A, Okojie C.E.E (2008) *Entrepreneurship Development: The Nigerian Experience*, Revised Ed. March Publishers, Nigeria.

Okafor F.C; Isenmila P.A; Inegbenebor A.U (2008) *Entrepreneurship A Practical Approach*, Mindex Publishing, Benin-City, Nigeria.

Hisrich R.D; Peter M.P; Shepherd D.A (2008) *Entrepreneurship*, McGraw-Hill, New York, USA.

Making All Things Happen Smartly
(*M.A.T.H.S*)

Why die in silence when you can relate with us for your business strategy, marketing strategy, leadership capacity building, corporate support services, seminars, business network meetings and media content programmes at Vinsage Consult.

Make the choice, do not compromise success.

Call Now: +234 703 085 5169, +234 812 298 6369

Email:sagevincentike@gmail.com,

vinsageconsult@yahoo.com

Facebook: Sage Vincent Ike

Twitter: Sage Vincent Ike

Google+: Sage Vincent Ikechukwu

ABOUT THE AUTHOR

Sage Vincent Ikechukwu is the principal consultant at Vinsage Consult, an entrepreneurial-cum-marketing communications consultancy with the vision to be the pre-eminent vehicle for enterprise engineering and value multiplied living in Africa and the Globe, under the corporate motto of **Making All Things Happen Smartly** (*M.A.T.H.S*).

The Sage as he is called is a corporate keynote speaker who is regularly invited to seminars, conferences, workshops and business network meetings to speak on entrepreneurship, leadership, motivation and productivity. As an entrepreneur consultant and a highly sought after creative content writer with interests in corporate strategy, marketing communications, innovations, public relations and human productivity, he has worked for several profitable small and medium scale businesses in the United States, Dubai-UAE, and African countries including South-Africa, Ghana, Tanzania and Nigeria.

Sage Vincent studied at the University of Learning with his highest education being the school of Inspiring experiences. He sits on the Board of a few corporate bodies. And as global citizen he speaks Chinese, English, Latin and Ibo languages appreciably. Sage Vincent Ikechukwu is satisfyingly married and blessed with children.

ABOUT THE BOOK

In this day and age, there is a special mandate to take up responsibility for our lives and be a part of the growing generation who are increasingly taking it upon themselves to chart a course and bring our world back to prosperity. In a world where the governments cannot create real jobs, you can implement your sellable ideas and create high-quality jobs in the system that drives the progress of humanity.

In this masterpiece, *Entrepreneur Guide*, Sage Vincent Ikechukwu shares with you the principles that will enable you go beyond organizing, managing and assuming the risks of a business or enterprise to develop what it takes to easily become very successful in a golden age.

Entrepreneur Guide will teach you how to discover the power in entrepreneurship and economic freedom, raise the capital you need to be in business and succeed in creating a position for yourself; creating an unprecedented source of wealth.

This is your time to start, manage and turn-around your business. This is your opportunity to take your place and come up with a brainwave so unique that others will pinch themselves for not having thought of it first. *Entrepreneur Guide* is a great read you need to make great strides in the entrepreneurial world.

www.ingramcontent.com/pod-product-compliance
Lightning Source LLC
Chambersburg PA
CBHW020155200326
41521CB00006B/380